PRISON BREAK

Studies in Postwar American Political Development

PRISON BREAK
Why Conservatives Turned Against Mass Incarceration

DAVID DAGAN AND STEVEN M. TELES

OXFORD
UNIVERSITY PRESS

OXFORD
UNIVERSITY PRESS

Oxford University Press is a department of the University of Oxford. It furthers
the University's objective of excellence in research, scholarship, and education
by publishing worldwide. Oxford is a registered trade mark of Oxford University
Press in the UK and certain other countries.

Published in the United States of America by Oxford University Press
198 Madison Avenue, New York, NY 10016, United States of America.

© Oxford University Press 2016

Library of Congress Cataloging-in-Publication Data
Names: Teles, Steven Michael, author. | Dagan, David.
Title: Prison break: how conservatives turned against mass incarceration /
Steven Teles, David Dagan.
Description: New York, NY: Oxford University Press, [2016] | Series: Studies in
post war american political development |
Includes bibliographical references and index.
Identifiers: LCCN 2016000684 (print) | LCCN 2016009349 (ebook) |
ISBN 978–0–19–024644–0 (hardback) | ISBN 978–0–19–024645–7 (E-book) |
ISBN 978–0–19–024646–4 (E-book)
Subjects: LCSH: Imprisonment—Political aspects—United States—History. |
Criminal justice, Administration of—Political aspects—United States—History. |
Conservatism—United States—History. | Political parties—Platforms—History. |
United States—Politics and government—History. |
BISAC: POLITICAL SCIENCE / Political Freedom & Security / Law Enforcement. |
POLITICAL SCIENCE / Political Freedom & Security / Human Rights. |
POLITICAL SCIENCE / Public Policy / Social Policy.
Classification: LCC HV9466 .T45 2016 (print) | LCC HV9466 (ebook) |
DDC 365/.973—dc23
LC record available at http://lccn.loc.gov/2016000684

9 8 7 6 5 4 3 2 1
Printed by Sheridan, USA

Contents

Acknowledgments

This book took longer than we originally thought it would, as our sense of what this project would become morphed from an article to an e-book to the study you hold in your hands. We owe a debt of gratitude to all the people who encouraged that evolution and helped get this book across the finish line. The Smith Richardson Foundation stepped up with a timely grant that helped us do the fieldwork for the cases. Olga Baranoff went above and beyond the call of duty, running down countless facts and getting the manuscript in shape. Mary Egan, Naomi Pitkin, Matt Varvaro, Gauri Wagle, and Christopher Winer also provided excellent research assistance. We thank Tim Bale, Frank Baumgartner, Angus Burgin, Alec Ewald, Stephen Farrall, Lauren Foley, Jacob Hacker, Angela Hawken, Alexander Hertel-Fernandez, Christopher Howard, David Karol, Mark Kleiman, Dylan Matthews, Lawrence Mead, Jesse Rhodes, Adam Sheingate, John Skrentny, Lester Spence, Chloe Thurston, and our two anonymous reviewers for all their feedback on the manuscript. Finally, David McBride, our editor at OUP, was enormously supportive in our effort to write a book for a broader audience.

A special thanks is due to our interviewees, who very generously shared their memories and, in some cases, documents from their private files. No book of this kind is possible unless those who participated in the events are willing to candidly comb through their past, often over the course of multiple interviews. We are also grateful to Michael Streepey of the National Association of State Budget Officers and Jonathan Woon of the University of Pittsburgh for sharing data with us.

Each of us has personal debts to pay. Both of us appreciate the patience of our spouses, Fawzia and Rebecca, who have busy careers of their own. We also ask forgiveness from our children—who were born during the course of this project—for the time that Daddy spent texting with his coauthor.

Steve would like to dedicate this book to his old friend and mentor, Glenn Loury. In one way or another, Steve and Glenn have been talking about intellectual themes that run through this book for two decades. He would also like to thank all of the folks at Open Philanthropy Project, for whom he did consulting on criminal justice during the time that this book was being written. That work helped him get perspective on the events described in the book that he might not have had as a mere academic.

David dedicates this book to his parents, Daniel and Sabine Dagan. Their affection for their new grandson reminds him daily of his own happy childhood.

Preface

Newt Gingrich had a war plan.

It was 1986. The overdose death of basketball star Len Bias had sent Washington into a full-blown drug panic. Gingrich, a Georgia congressman, was circulating a memo calling for an assault on illegal narcotics on the scale of World War II—"a decisive, all-out effort to destroy the underground drug empire."[1]

An "incremental" approach such as the gradual American escalation in Vietnam would be doomed to failure, Gingrich argued. Americans would not tolerate another long grind. They would back the drug war only if it was massive and swift—aiming at victory within three years. His conclusion: "We must focus the total resources necessary to win a decisive victory. One too many won't be a big waste. One too few will lead to defeat."[2]

Gingrich never got a World War II–sized mobilization. But as it turned out, Americans did have an appetite for a protracted war against drugs and crime, and Gingrich repeatedly pushed to give that war a political front. In 1988, as an advisor to the presidential campaign of George H. W. Bush, Gingrich declared that the Democratic nominee, Michael Dukakis, had "a kind of attitude on crime which puts the innocent citizen at risk and which favors the crim-inal."[3] The following year, Gingrich urged Republicans to pound on the crime theme in congressional races.[4]

Gingrich's close ally Grover Norquist also saw the political potential in the crime war. As the antitax activist argued in 1993, the waning of the Soviet threat had reduced Americans' hunger for tough leadership—a key Republican advantage. But, Norquist argued, "as the worldwide struggle against Soviet imperialism faded, another issue began to emerge that might well replace it in the conservative arsenal: crime." Just as Democrats had been unable to stand up to the Soviets, Norquist wrote, they were incapable of taking "a sensible stand on stiff sentencing and more prisons."[5]

By this point, the United States had already shattered incarceration records, caging its citizens at a higher rate than any other democracy on Earth.[6] In the summer of 1994, the Democratic Congress doubled down by passing a crime bill that provided billions of dollars in federal aid for building more prisons. It wasn't enough for Gingrich, however. His famous "Contract with America" promised "cuts in social spending from this summer's 'crime' bill to fund prison construction and additional law enforcement."[7] That fall, the GOP took control of the House of Representatives, making Gingrich the first Republican Speaker since the 1950s.[8]

Gingrich and his allies would later shut down the government in a drive to impose fiscal austerity. All the same, they passed legislation that would have given states even more prison funding and made sentences even longer than the 1994 bill did.[9] The war on crime had turned out to be long, not short. But the logic of Gingrich's 1986 memo—"one too many won't be a big waste"—still applied.

Until now.

In 2011, Norquist spoke at a Washington briefing on criminal justice advertised as attacking conservatives' "Last Sacred Cow." For years, Norquist said, conservatives were too busy rolling back frivolous government operations to worry about the workings of essentials such as crime control. But conservatives could no longer afford to direct their critique of government only at their traditional targets. "Spending more on education doesn't necessarily get you more education. We know that—that's obvious. Well, that's also true about national defense. That's also true about criminal justice and fighting crime."[10]

At the same time, Gingrich, now 25 years removed from his drug-war memo, was also striking a decidedly new tone. "There is an urgent need to address the astronomical growth in the prison population, with its huge costs in dollars and lost human potential," he declared in 2011. "The criminal-justice system is broken, and conservatives must lead the way in fixing it."[11]

Activists such as Norquist and Gingrich have decided that caging Americans should become a solution of last resort, not the default approach to crime. "Stiff sentencing and more prisons" has turned into "smart sentencing and less incarceration." Conservatives once treated "criminal justice" as exempt from their critique of big government. They took their cues on sentencing from police and prosecutors and didn't think twice about building more prisons and expanding the crime-control apparatus. Many of those same conservatives, and their successors, are now lining up to challenge the value of incarceration and express sympathy for those behind bars.

Skeptics might detect more than a whiff of opportunism in these pronouncements, coming in an era when crime is no longer the hot issue it once was and when recessions have battered state finances like never before. But conservatives themselves have contributed substantially to de-escalating the nation's crime debate over the last decade. And if conservatives now think incarceration is too expensive, it's partly because they no longer see it delivering much benefit.

A dramatic example of the new conservative take on criminal justice is Rick Perry, the former governor of Texas and two-time presidential candidate. When Republicans in the Texas legislature pushed a series of reforms to curtail the state's prison population in 2005 and 2007, Perry offered lukewarm support at best.

By 2015, however, Perry had embraced the cause of corrections reform, citing it as a signature accomplishment and a reason that African American voters should take his second presidential candidacy seriously. "One of the most important things we did in Texas while I was governor is reform our drug-related sentencing laws, so that nonviolent offenders could stay out of prison," he said. Perry made the case for "second chances and human redemption," declaring, "Americans who suffer from an addiction need help, not moral condemnation. By treating alcohol and drug abuse as a disease, we have given Texans who have experienced a run-in with the law the help they need and the rehabilitation that many seek." He promised that if he was elected president, "We can reform federal sentencing laws—just as we have done at the state level—to ensure more young people have a shot at a better life."[12] In fact, most of the 2016 presidential contenders endorsed some type of sentencing reform.[13]

As more Republicans in the states undergo conversions like Perry's, and more of the arbiters of conservative orthodoxy such as Gingrich and Norquist embrace the cause of reform, reducing mass incarceration inches ever closer to official Republican Party doctrine. It is a remarkable and unexpected retreat from what was once a conservative article of faith. And it is a breakthrough that has opened the door to the most significant sentencing reform movement America has seen in decades.

This book will explain how it came about. As we show, the decline of public anxiety about crime and a newly anti-statist mood in the Republican Party provided an opening for reformers to change minds. But to make good on this opportunity, those conservatives, and their allies outside the movement, had to slowly build a reform cadre designed to convince Republicans that being indiscriminately tough on crime was not the appropriate position for conservatives, and that reducing sentences and emphasizing reentry was.

Our story sheds light on the way that information is processed in a hyper-partisan era, and how that shapes the opportunities for major policy change in our polarized political environment. Our political system is no longer capable of coming to agreement on great political questions by splitting the difference or logrolling behind closed doors. There is little prospect that major policy changes will happen because of the power of expert opinion and evidence.[14] Changing policy in the coming decades, except in rare moments when one party has complete control, means changing minds—convincing the arbiters of ideological orthodoxy that they need to shift position for their own reasons. Understanding when such changes are possible, and how they come about, is central to our ability to do politics effectively in an era when our older techniques for generating consensus have broken down.

In no other case during the era of polarization has one of our political parties changed so thoroughly, and so suddenly, as Republicans have on criminal justice. We would do well to understand precisely why and how this change occurred if we have any hope of making similar breakthroughs in the future.

PRISON BREAK

CHAPTER 1

How Minds Change

Almost everyone can recall things that we once firmly believed but that we now think are wrong.[1] We explain these changes by saying that we know things now that we did not know then. That is, we tell ourselves a story of our evolution in which our ideas are sensitive to new information. We tinker, we try things out, we engage in trial and error, and eventually we reach the right position. This is a part of how we understand ourselves to be "rational."

Social science tells a different story, however. Our positions on social and political questions are shaped as much by who we think we are—our identity—as by what we know.[2] Once we have established the positions that seem appropriate for the kind of person we imagine ourselves to be, we cling to them like a spider to its web. Our beliefs become an important part of how we think of ourselves and how we are viewed by others.

Because we become invested in the positions we hold, most of us filter out or struggle to discredit information that would make our beliefs seem suspect.[3] We cluster together with other people who share our beliefs and avoid those who do not. When we do change our minds, it is less because a new piece of information is hot off the presses, and more because old information has suddenly become the "kind of thing that a person like me pays attention to." When people we trust to be guardians of our identity announce that our current positions are problematic, we may be willing to take account of things we previously ignored and to shift accordingly.[4]

Conservatives, as the preface showed, are changing their minds on criminal justice. They are not doing so because new information has suddenly emerged.[5] In fact, compelling evidence on cost, recidivism, and the racial disparities of mass incarceration has been available for well over two decades, but only recently have conservatives paid attention to it. Consider:

Cost: Between 1977 and 2003, state and local spending on corrections grew twice as fast as health care and education spending and 50 percent more than welfare spending.[6] Skeptics argued throughout the 1980s that these costs were unsustainable but were stymied by the argument that, like national defense, there was no price too high to pay for public safety.[7] Things are different today: cost is now one of the primary justifications that conservatives invoke for prison reform.

Recidivism: High recidivism rates are now being seen as evidence of prison's inefficacy—but these data are not new either. In 1989, the Bureau of Justice Statistics published a study of 16,000 inmates in eleven states. Within three years of their release, almost two-thirds had been rearrested for a serious offense. The results appeared in the nation's leading newspapers—albeit as briefs—but were mentioned just once in the *Congressional Record*.[8] Some states followed up with recidivism studies of their own. Proposals to increase funding for programs to battle the problem, or even to tie Corrections Departments' funding to performance on this front, were also floated on occasion.[9] But the nation's chief crime-control policy through the 1990s continued to be the construction of more prisons.[10] Today, conservatives frequently invoke high recidivism rates as evidence that the money Americans are spending on prisons is being wasted.[11] A 2011 report reprised the grim state of recidivism at a level of detail that had not previously been available, but the new data did not suggest that the problem had gotten worse than it had been 20 years before.[12]

Racial disparity: The racial skew in American incarceration rates has been well documented and thoroughly debated since at least the turn of the century.[13] Evidence that the war on drugs was worsening the situation accumulated during the 1980s and 1990s and was underscored by a handful of high-profile reports.[14] As John DiIulio, a student of the prominent conservative James Q. Wilson and longtime advocate of tougher sentencing, wrote in 1989, "Nobody denies that as America's corrections population has skyrocketed, the non-white proportion has reached historic highs."[15] The *Wall Street Journal* observed in 1989, "Incarceration no doubt also means jailing a disproportionate number of minority youth," but concluded grimly that "fighting drugs isn't a dainty job."[16]

Today, most conservative prison reformers do not go out of their way to highlight racial disparities, but neither do they appear complacent about the issue, and they are paying increasing attention. The leading conservative reform group, Right on Crime, has done publicity work together with the NAACP. Kentucky Senator Rand Paul has gone so far as to compare mass incarceration to Jim Crow, and some conservative commentators have argued that taking up prison reform could help the party in its quest to make inroads with minorities.[17] More recently, a senior aide to the libertarian mega-funders Charles and David Koch has observed that American criminal justice "definitely appears to have a racial angle, intended or not" and, more strikingly, "We have more of America now in prison than they ever did (in South Africa) in apartheid ... Let that swirl around in your head for a while."[18]

While the basic facts about mass incarceration have not changed much, what *has* changed is that conservatives have become more willing to absorb that information, thanks to a newfound sense that doing so is appropriate for people like them. To understand how this change happened, we need to start by looking at the complex mix of identity, strategy, persuasion, and calculation that causes social movements and parties to develop—and change—the positions they hold. Only then can we understand the politics that culminates in partisans being told by leaders they trust that it is permissible, even morally obligatory, to change their minds.

THINKING ABOUT THINKING

We all have an image in our mind of what rational thinking looks like. We start out with a position that incorporates all the information that we have available to us. We act on that position, thereby changing the world and generating new information, which may confirm our original expectations or contradict them. We process this information and then update our position accordingly.

What gets in the way of this highly rational ideal is that our emotions and reputations become wrapped up with the positions that we take. We seek out information that reinforces our beliefs and pay close attention when it is presented to us. Conversely, we go out of our way, even without noticing it, to avoid information that would challenge our convictions, and we find ways to ignore or explain it away when it is presented to us.[19] When you play out this process of selective attention over and over again, the effect is to reinforce our existing commitments. Psychologists call this process "confirmation bias."

Confirmation bias is reinforced by the fact that identity is essentially collective. Group attachments form a key part of how we understand ourselves and present ourselves to others. Position-taking is an important ritual of group membership, in which we declare who we are by announcing what we think. Consequently, when people develop their positions on various public issues, they ask themselves, fundamentally, "What is it that a person like me is supposed to think on this question?" before they pay close attention to the facts.[20]

HOW POLICYMAKERS THINK

This process is not limited to the uninformed or unintelligent. In fact, there is suggestive experimental evidence that motivated reasoning is *more* common among the conceptually sophisticated.[21] An ideological framework takes time, training, and energy to develop, which is why we have long known that the strength of such frameworks increases with more education.[22] Ideology and partisanship profoundly shape how people process information, leading to deep and durable differences in what members of rival teams believe about even relatively straightforward facts.[23]

This effect is likely to be even stronger for politicians in that their "group" is not just experienced in the vicarious, media-filtered way that many of us define our attachments. Instead, the beliefs of the group are something that politicians experience as coming from people whom they know personally, and whom they consider to be part of their emotional and material support system—people whose success is intimately connected to their own.

In a previous age, politicians identified both with ideological movements—primarily conservatism or liberalism—and with political parties. These commitments of ideology and partisanship were often at odds, moderating the effect of group identity. That is much less true today, given that the two American political parties are far more polarized than they have been in almost a century.[24] Party and ideological instincts no longer conflict but reinforce one another. Polarization means that the intensity of emotional aversion to the "other" side—and the information that comes from there—is much hotter than it has been in previous eras, when the "other side" was a constantly shifting coalition rather than a target with a party label.[25] As a result, politicians are much more likely to get their ideas and information from ideologically sorted sources, such as partisan media, think tanks, and interest groups.[26] While identity has always been a core part of politicians' information processing, therefore, the strength of their group attachments and the price for straying from the herd are stronger than ever.

The consequence of this increasing ideological sorting is that additional empirical "evidence" on any contested matter is highly unlikely, in and of itself, to change anyone's mind. Take the issue of human-generated climate change. Almost all climate scientists consider the threshold question in the debate (is global warming real, caused by human action, and creating serious threats to human life) settled. When faced with policymakers who do not accept these beliefs, researchers might bemoan their scientific illiteracy, or simply throw more and more information at them. But none of these responses seems to do anything except harden the beliefs of those on the other side. The more scientists work together to spread their findings, the more conservative skeptics perceive them as driven by ideology rather than facts. In fact, even Republicans who previously recognized the imperative to act, such as Senator John McCain, have since joined the skeptics under pressure not to stray from the partisan herd.[27]

On issues without strong cultural or ideological resonance, expert opinion and information may actually help change policymakers' minds. Most issues of substantial significance, however, are already sorted into ideological categories by policymakers—and it's getting worse.[28] Issues that in the past were considered to be "non-partisan," such as infrastructure and the environment, are increasingly characterized by single-party coalitions.[29]

In sum, we should expect the positions of policymakers to be very stable, even in the face of new information. But we also know that they *do* change. In fact, this entire book is about one very important example of such change. So how do policymakers, whose minds are fortified with such cognitive and organizational barriers to new information, come to embrace facts that they once shunned? Why do they adopt positions that they once abhorred?

OPENING MINDS

If scientific information on its own cannot change the minds of ideologically entrenched policymakers, what can? Important work by Yale's Dan Kahan and his collaborators shows that our group-based, emotional reactions do not need to be *suppressed* in order to make us open to new information—they need to be *satisfied*. Before individuals can process a particular piece of information, they need to believe it does not represent a threat to identity. The information must be understood as the kind of thing that people like them believe, which means that the identity of the messenger matters a great deal. For instance, Kahan and Braman showed that respondents reacted very differently to a proposal for an HPV vaccine depending on the character of the expert making the claim.[30] They refer to the use of trusted messengers as "identity vouching," because people we see as members of our team "vouch" that the information in question is no threat to our group identity.

Identity vouching is most likely to be successful when public figures of "high esteem within their cultural or ideological group" support a challenge to movement orthodoxy.[31] As a result of their status, people of high esteem can address the contradictions that inevitably crop up in any movement of distinctive factions held together by an attachment to broad principles. These identity vouchers can argue that they are simply applying those foundational principles in novel combinations, or to issues that had previously been overlooked. "People of high esteem" can also include leaders so honored because they hold a professional position that, in the view of a particular culture, makes their opinions on a particular subject seem highly credible. The most obvious example is a former four-star general offering his opinion on military strategy. Such people are rendered all the more credible when they appear to be making an argument that violates their self-interest.[32]

Identity vouching does not come easy, however. Even people of high esteem cannot change entrenched beliefs with a mere snap of the fingers. The process requires organization and commitment. It happens in the real world, in the actual flow of political events—not in a lab. Building a successful campaign of identity-vouching is a process that is rational, opportunistic, resource intensive, and strategic. The process is rational because movement contrarians must identify prospective allies and target them in the right forums. This depends on what we call, in chapter 4, "relationships." It is opportunistic because persuading fellow movement adherents to change their minds may depend on linking the new position to a shift in conditions or unexpected events, allowing the activist to obscure that a shift in position has actually occurred. The process is resource intensive because identifying the right politicians, packaging information in ways that appeal to them, and reframing political interest requires manpower, time, and access. Finally, it is strategic because attempts at identity vouching will be met with resistance from others in the same cultural group, requiring well-placed counter-moves and crafty adjustments to the tactics deployed by the defenders of the status quo.

In other words, people who generally perceive themselves to be on the same team will find themselves at odds over the meaning of their shared values when a process of identity vouching is initiated. As the campaign unleashes dormant frictions, the movement enters a period of uncertainty, in which once-consensual positions are suddenly up for grabs. In such an environment, winners need more than material resources. They need intangible skills such as motivation, salient knowledge, trust, creativity, and the ability to learn on the fly.[33] In short, they need political skill, or what Machiavelli called *virtù*.

Political science provides another way to think about what it takes to mount a successful identity-vouching campaign. Scholars of the policymaking process have found that most policies enjoy long periods of stability until a sudden flurry of attention, often panicked in tone, leads to an influx of new actors who produce radical change. When policies are stable, they are cemented by supportive institutional arrangements and, critical for our account, an attractive policy image. A policy image is much like a brand. It

amounts to a sense that the policy is either working or failing, and it is closely tied to the reputation of the people at
the wheel. When that image is disrupted, enormous change
can happen in a very short period of time, as in the rapid
decline in support for nuclear energy in the wake of the
1979 accident at Three Mile Island.[34]

Motivated cognition can play a very powerful role in
the creation and destruction of policy images. On the way
"up," a positive policy image will cause observers to ignore
negative information and pay excessive attention to positive
information. That further reinforces policy image, thereby
leading to even more biased cognition. But the same process operates in the other direction. Once the reputation of
a policy has been damaged, it can kick off a vicious cycle, in
which evidence of positive functioning is ignored and even
ambivalent signals are weighed negatively. The art of policy
entrepreneurship in this area, therefore, is to create a policy
cascade by "tipping" the cognitive process from virtuous
to vicious, from reinforcement to stigma.[35] This process
occurs largely *prior* to the rational assessment of evidence. It
determines what evidence the actors focus on, what additional evidence they seek to collect, and how they process
what they find.

Identity vouching operates in two channels, with two
distinct audiences. The process begins with a very small
core group of movement leaders that has decided that their
group's position needs to change, often for deeply held
moral and personal reasons. They then seek to change the
positions of the larger group of highly visible, ideologically
unassailable movement leaders. This process typically occurs
behind the scenes, and it depends crucially on *relationships*.
The core group of movement leaders have typically been
through numerous battles together and have developed
strong ties between each other. The would-be identity

vouchers must leverage these relationships to convert the remaining trustees of the movement's brand. Once the elite cadre has been substantially converted, they can then communicate the change of position to the larger group of movement adherents—including legislators and the general public—relying on their *reputation* for ideological purity. They will typically explain the reasons for a switch with reference to the movement's deeper cultural commitments. At the end of this sequence, movement activists and affiliated politicians will be open to information they had previously feared as a threat to identity.

STRATEGY AND STRUCTURE

Would-be reformers do not face a completely open field for changing the minds of their co-partisans, however. While art, skill, and charisma are very important to this process, much depends on forces over which purveyors of policy change have little control. These are the structural or contextual factors that are akin to what Machiavelli called *fortuna*: changes that an activist can prepare for and respond to, but not generate in the first place. Ultimately, position change is generated by a combination of skill and structure.

In understanding the structural constraints and opportunities for policy change, it is useful to think of two kinds of issues. The first is what we can call "coalitionally rooted" issues, ones where party members have a position because a deeply mobilized, core constituency in their partisan team insists on it. For example, the pro-life and anti–gun control policies in the Republican Party surely reflect the genuine beliefs of party elites. But they are anchored by the recognition that if the party was to change its position on those issues, pro-life activists and the NRA might yank their support, with disastrous consequences. So even if those issues are not working in attracting votes—in some cases, even if they are proving *counterproductive* at the ballot box—they are still immune to change unless leaders in the party coalition are willing to jettison those core groups. For obvious reasons, this is something that rarely happens. One example is the decision by key leaders of the Democratic Party to risk the loss of Southern segregationists by backing federal civil rights laws, a choice that was itself a product of the party's prior decision to incorporate black voters into its coalition. By and large, however, coalitionally entrenched positions are not a very promising place to encourage change.[36]

Most of the questions politicians confront are not like abortion and gun control. They are what David Karol has called "groupless" issues. On these issues, a party adopts a position in order to opportunistically capture votes from the electorate at large, rather than to please an organized member of its coalition.[37] There will certainly be interest groups who care a great deal about these issues and will seek to prevent party position change. But they will not be groups who define the party's core constituency and who have a seat at the very small table where party decisions are made. These sorts of issues are much more attractive for entrepreneurs trying to change party positions, but they come with their own challenges.

For example, when a policy is widely perceived to be a successful vote-getter, the movement may find it difficult to notice its unexpected or pathological consequences on the ground. Policymakers are unlikely to be very interested in the downsides of a policy when they are actively using it on the campaign trail to attack their opponents, or when it continues to be strongly and intensely supported by the public. On the other hand, when public attention shifts or the underlying problem is perceived to have been fixed, those same policymakers may be willing to consider changing their position. Policy entrepreneurs can influence these hardball political considerations at the margins, but they are best understood as *fortuna*, an environmental situation beyond their control.

Moreover, just because an issue is "groupless" in the sense that there is no mass constituency rallied behind it does not mean positions on it are easy to change. Policymakers may still firmly believe the stands they have previously taken are right. As we show in the next chapter, the "tough on crime" posture became deeply embedded in the Republican Party because it was electorally successful, but also ideologically seductive and emotionally motivating.

Policymakers also care far more about their reputation for consistency than do ordinary members of the public. Changing positions can expose a politician to ridicule as a "flip-flopper" and raise questions about her credibility. In order to convince policymakers that it is safe to change their position, a rhetorical framework must be developed in which they can do so while claiming they were right all along. For example, policymakers might argue that "the character of the problem has changed" or "the success of the policy we advanced now renders it unnecessary," but relatively rarely will they admit, "We screwed up." For the same reason, generational change can make party position change easier. Newer politicians have less psychological or reputational investment in the policy than those who set it on its current course, and thus an easier time changing direction.

Changing minds is, therefore, a process that needs to happen from the inside out. Only actors with status within an ideological movement can do the work of getting their co-partisans to pay attention to ideas that they once thought of as "beyond the pale." But that does not mean that actors outside the movement are irrelevant to the process we are describing. Far from it. In the story that we tell in the chapters to come, especially chapter 5, we will see that outsiders can play a critical role. They can provide vital financial subsidy, at least when they do so carefully and quietly, so as not to tar the cause with the mark of ideological deviance. They can generate intelligence, vet policy alternatives, and do the analytical grunt work required to get a policy right, once the decision makers are persuaded to change. They can do all that only when they recognize, however, that they need to seem—and up to a point, actually *be*—in a subordinate role to ideological insiders.

Changing minds is a difficult, complicated business. Even on issues where the status quo is vulnerable, it takes a combination of resources, strategy, organization, and helpful allies to alter longstanding beliefs. Twenty years ago, few observers would have predicted that such a shift in party positions was possible in the case of crime. The chapters to come will explain how it happened, and why.

CHAPTER 2

The Rise of Law and Order Conservatism

> The important thing to know about Southern California
> is that the people who live there, who grew up there, love
> it. Not just the way one has an attachment to a home-
> town, any hometown, but the way people love the real-
> ization that they have found the right mode of life.[1]
> James Q. Wilson, "A Guide to Reagan Country,"
> *Commentary*, 1967

Pat Nolan's boyhood on Crenshaw Boulevard in 1950s
Los Angeles could have been perfect.

The sixth of nine children, Nolan was born into a
middle-class, Catholic family that looked like that of
hundreds of thousands of other Angelenos. His father
was an accountant who moved west from Nashville as
a child, his mother a fourth-generation Californian and
homemaker.

Pat had a paper route and served as an altar boy at
the family's church, St. Paul's. Occasionally, the Nolans
hopped on the streetcar for a day at the beach. They spot-
ted Hollywood stars at restaurants that ordinary Angelenos
like themselves could afford to dine at. And sometimes, Pat

would simply lay in their backyard and stare into the cloud-less blue sky.

"It was an idyllic place," Nolan recalls.[2]

All was not well in that sunny idyll, however. Nolan witnessed the beginnings of the Crenshaw neighbor-hood's transition from middle-class enclave to violent ghetto. A boy who lived four doors down was killed by a shotgun blast. One of Pat's brothers had his wrists slashed in a mugging. Another walked into the pharmacy where he worked one day to find the aftermath of a robbery—the elderly owners gagged and bound to an overhead pipe.[3] Crenshaw would eventually be known as a cradle of gangsta rap and one of the areas hardest hit by the 1992 Los Angeles riots.

Crime had become a threat to the "mode of life" that Angelenos like the Nolan family thought was their birth-right. The militant defense of that Southern California promise would later become the backbone of the region's distinctive conservatism, and a driving force in the trans-formation of conservatism nationwide.[4]

When Pat was 11, the family moved to suburban Burbank—joining the waves of white flight that hollowed out American cities from coast to coast. Pat joined the Police Explorers, a group for kids interested in law-enforcement careers, and threw himself into the family's conservative politics. The Nolans had been fans of Barry Goldwater since 1960, when the conservative *National Review* began touting the Arizona senator's ideas. Pat's father became a Goldwater precinct captain during the senator's insurgent bid for the 1964 Republican presidential nomination, a campaign that was decided largely in the battleground of California.

Pat followed the path enthusiastically. He joined a chapter of the conservative youth organization Young Americans for Freedom at his high school. In 1966, he started a Youth for Reagan chapter in Burbank to support the actor's winning gubernatorial bid. He went to college at the University of Southern California and established a Young Americans for Freedom presence there, too. The movement was small in those days, and Pat quickly made friends with future Reagan aides Edwin Meese and Lyn Nofziger; conservative editor Stan Evans; and like-minded young conservatives such as David Keene, who one day would become president of the National Rifle Association and the American Conservative Union.[5]

In 1976, Nolan worked on Ronald Reagan's first presidential campaign. Two years later, at the tender age of 28, he made his own bid for office, running for a seat in the California Assembly. He and a slate of like-minded Republicans were powered to victory that fall amid a property-tax revolt that had brought Californians to the polls in a conservative mood.

Nolan wasted no time making a name for himself in Sacramento. He became the leader of a group of legislators so conservative they were nicknamed the "cavemen."[6] In 1984, he rose to the leadership of the Assembly's Republican caucus, toppling the moderate incumbent after a bitter power struggle.

Despite his ambition and unblinking ideology, Nolan was well liked. He wore a kilt into the Assembly chamber on St. Patrick's Day and talked about the Los Angeles Rams with anybody who would listen. He had the charisma to go further. There were whispers that a run for attorney general could be next.

He was, the *Sacramento Bee* declared, "the arch-conservative boy wonder."[7]

Nolan used his clout to help drive a revolution in criminal justice. Close with the law-enforcement community and trusted by Republican Gov. George Deukmejian, Nolan took a lead role in legislation that added more than a dozen new prisons to the California system, including the notorious "supermax" lockup at Pelican Bay.[8] In the process, he helped drive a period of conservative ascendancy in California that led the voters to elect a Republican to the governorship for 24 out of 32 years, from 1966 to 1998.[9]

Like many conservatives, Nolan occasionally found room for subtlety in his views on crime. Mindful of the young people he knew back in Crenshaw who had gone astray, he pushed for restorative approaches to juvenile justice. But the dominant message, for both Nolan and his movement, was a hawkish one: "the liberals were all wet . . . their policies were leading to the breakdown of neighborhoods and crime was really corrupting."[10]

It was no accident that the heir apparent to California's conservative revolution was also a leading advocate of law-and-order politics. At the same time as the Nolan family fled Los Angeles and Pat made friends on the Burbank police force, the idea that crime should be met with an iron fist was sinking into the bedrock of conservative politics.

By the 1980s, being tough on crime had become a core part of what it meant to *be* a conservative. That created a powerful motivation for conservatives to embrace evidence that "prison works," and to discount warning signs that incarceration was getting out of control. Before we can understand how the relationship between crime and conservative identity is changing, we need to understand how it was forged in the first place.

THE SCHISM OF THE '60S

The modern crime war began during Nolan's boyhood, when a series of transformations shook the American party system and the conservative movement.

Since the New Deal, the two major political parties had polarized sharply, with the Democrats claiming the territory of representing the working and middle class—ensuring the security of their jobs, their retirement, their neighborhoods. With economic security as the central axis of American politics, the Democrats possessed a fundamental, structural advantage—one that put the Republicans, as Samuel Lubell observed in 1951, playing the moon to the Democrats' sun.[11] They could sometimes win national races, but they did not determine the terms of politics.

The success of the civil rights movement was the first major crack in this party system. Many Southern segregationists broke with the Democratic Party, even running Strom Thurmond as their own "Dixiecrat" candidate for president in 1948. With the "Solid South" coming unglued, Republicans started to imagine new ways that politics could be put back together in a way that gave Republicans the durable advantage that Democrats once held. In time, the South would become undisputed GOP territory, a trend illustrated by Thurmond himself: the Dixiecrat of the '40s and '50s became a powerful Republican in the 1960s.[12]

Across the nation, the black freedom struggle left many whites who had embraced the Democrats' promises of "security" feeling deeply unsettled. In the South, they were rattled by the demise of segregation; in the North, by challenges to the racial composition of neighborhoods, busing of schoolchildren, and blacks' increasing demands to assert political control of cities.[13] North and South, Republicans claimed that they would defend the interests of ordinary white working people who had been abandoned by the Democrats.

The new racial tensions spawned by the victory over segregation were aggravated by broader attacks on traditional American social structures. College campuses that Americans had previously looked to with pride were roiled by protests and even violence—as with the 1969 building takeovers at Cornell—and the uproar was met by what seemed like a reluctance to enforce basic rules.[14] More broadly, authorities of all sorts seemed to be losing control—of kids using drugs, of pornography and lewdness in popular culture, of women abandoning traditional standards of femininity. American parents worried that their children would succumb to the forces of indecency, a fear encapsulated by the kidnapping of Patty Hearst—the good girl who ended up with a rifle in her hands.[15]

These anxieties were exacerbated by a rapid increase in violent crime, best illustrated by homicides.[16] As Figure 2-1 shows, in 1960, the American murder rate was 5.1 per 100,000; by 1980 it had doubled to 10.2. The numbers for Nolan's California were 3.9 in 1960 and a terrifying 14.5 in 1980 (see Figure 2-I).

In California and across the nation, families were living out the Nolans' Crenshaw experience, or fearing that they were next. Even where they did not actually witness crime, middle-class white Americans saw that standards of order in urban parks, schools, and city streets were slipping. They began to abandon cities, but moving did not eliminate their fears. Even more frightening than what had already

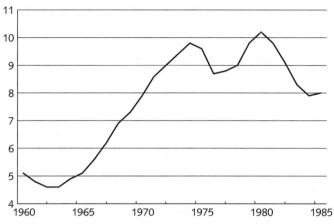

Figure 2-1 U.S. Murders per 100,000 People, 1960–1985.
Source: FBI, Uniform Crime Reports, prepared by the National Archive of Criminal Justice Data, 2015.

happened was the possibility that crime could keep getting worse, spreading out of the "inner cities" into the white, middle-class suburbs. In Richard Nixon's ominous warning: "The brutal society that now flourishes in the core cities of America will annex the affluent suburbs."[17] That, as much as anything, was the force that drove the crime and drug panics, the fear that the civilizational collapse of once-great American cities would suck in the children of those who managed to escape.[18]

Perceptions of social disintegration were also reinforced by popular movies featuring stories of warped, deranged criminals who would get away with murder but for the intervention of a Clint Eastwood or Charles Bronson— heroes forced to operate on the margins of a social system that had lost its spine.[19] These anti-liberal heroes showed that there was abundant demand for a blunt, unsympathetic, no-nonsense response to social disorder, a template that politicians quickly caught on to.

THE RHETORIC OF DISORDER

The combination of a civil-rights breakthrough, revolutionary student politics, and rapidly spiking crime gave Republicans plenty of kindling with which to enflame the passions of conservative white voters. To take advantage of this moment, many Republicans drew on rhetorical strategies originally deployed by segregationist Southern Democrats. Playing on the fears of racists that criminal impulses were innate to African Americans, defenders of the Jim Crow order had long argued there was an intimate connection between integration and rising crime. As early as World War II, segregationist politicians pointed to race riots that shook relatively integrated Northern cities as evidence that mixing of the races would lead to the victimization of whites by blacks.[20]

As the civil rights movement crested, these attacks became more pointed. Southern conservatives alleged that the movement itself was responsible for violence, either by directly instigating riots or by using civil disobedience to undermine the authority of the law. In 1959, Thurmond warned that "political demands for integration of the races" would produce a "wave of terror, crime, and juvenile delinquency."[21]

As practiced by Southern Democrats, such rhetoric linking racial equality with disorder did not have a promising future. Too powerful was the moral authority of the civil rights movement, too decisive the national consensus against the crude bigotry of the South. The Goldwater campaign of 1964 showed the way forward by more artfully linking street crime, rioting, and civil rights.[22] His references to civil rights were more abstract, allowing his audience to fill in the blanks. Thus, he argued that the more the federal government "has attempted to legislate morality, the more it actually has incited hatreds and violence."[23] In an allusion that conflated demonstrators with rioters and criminals, Goldwater pinned the blame for rising crime on those "have gone to the streets to seek with violence what can only be found in understanding."[24] The riots that scorched the nation's cities after 1964 made this conflation an easy sell.

Ronald Reagan emulated Goldwater in his successful run for California governor in 1966, using the Watts riot and unrest at Berkeley to bludgeon the liberal incumbent, Pat Brown. Two years later, Richard Nixon rode the same strategy all the way to the White House. In his speech accepting the Republican nomination, Nixon declared: "Let those who have the responsibility to enforce our laws and our judges who have the responsibility to interpret them be dedicated to the great principles of civil rights. But let them also recognize that the first civil right of every American is to be free from domestic violence, and that right must be guaranteed in this country."[25] That "but" was an echo of the segregationist warnings, suggesting that the civil rights movement had somehow undermined what Nixon called "the first civil right."[26]

Crime rhetoric was thus loaded with racial appeals, but in order to work, it had to be scrubbed of overt racism. As political scientist Tali Mendelberg has written, "When a society has repudiated racism, yet racial conflict persists, candidates can win by playing the race card only through implicit racial appeals."[27] In moments of candor, Republican leaders acknowledged this reality. Richard Nixon reportedly told a confidante, "[T]he whole problem is really the blacks. The key is to devise a system that recognizes this while not appearing to."[28]

This framework was not merely a "sanitization" of Southern segregationist language. It was a genuinely new creation in which crime became the outlet not just for racial tensions, but for a wide range of fears. Civil rights, campus protest, changing gender mores, and other upheavals were all cast as elements of a broader social breakdown that manifested itself in violence. Goldwater and his successors wove a political narrative that combined all of these— above all, the fear of victimization—under the broad theme of *disorder.*

Reagan's fulminations over the turmoil at UC-Berkeley in 1966 became a leading example of how this cocktail was to be mixed. He warned that an appearance on campus of civil-rights activist Stokely Carmichael would bring on racial violence; claimed (with wild exaggeration) that a campus dance had descended into an orgy; and chastised the sitting governor, Pat Brown, for not having grabbed upstart students "by the scruff of the neck and thrown them off campus—personally."[29] In the vision of conservatism that Reagan impressed on the Republican Party, limiting the expansion of civil rights was woven into a larger web of anxieties about liberation run amuck.

The drug scares of the 1980s lent a desperate, even existential tone to the warnings of criminal ascendance. For example, Carlton Turner, the director of the Drug Abuse Policy Office in the Reagan administration (the precursor to the "drug czar") argued in 1986 that "When a user buys marijuana or cocaine, he or she is financing our nation's suicide ... Drug dollars go to criminals who are determined to destroy our country ... This is not a rights issue; this is a survival issue."[30] There was a parallel between the Cold War and the War on Drugs. Both would be won by taking a forceful stand, not by accommodation.

The sharp end of the conservative spear was the claim that in the battle against "the criminal forces" in society, the ruling liberal elite was on the side of the bad guys. Social authority was being undermined, conservatives alleged, with the acquiescence of the establishment: bleeding-heart academics who blamed crime on "root causes," naive judges who swaddled thugs in the technicalities of legal procedure, university presidents who folded before the mobs overrunning campuses, and spineless politicians who refused to stand up for common decency. In other words, the crime wave besetting Americans was the product of a dangerous alliance between the violent rabble on the one hand and the arrogant establishment on the other.

Nixon, for example, warned that "some of our courts in their decisions have gone too far in weakening the peace forces as against the criminal forces in this country."[31] Reagan, meanwhile, declared that criminals were "a new privileged class," and judicial lenience meant repeat offenders could be "confident that once their cases enter our legal system the charges will be dropped, postponed, plea-bargained away or lost in a maze of legal technicalities."[32] This argument formed a bridge to subsequent critiques of welfare, which increasingly was cast as a blank check the privileged classes wrote to the nation's cadgers, to be cashed from the accounts of America's hard-working middle class.[33]

Crime, race, and disorder were thus meshed together with arguments against the welfare state to form a powerful way of reconceptualizing the American class structure. No longer was the dividing line in American life between the Bosses (protected by the Republicans) and the Working Class (defended by the Democrats). It was between those who upheld the social order and those who tore it down.[34] This frame elided the easy division of "social" and "economic" issues. Instead, it cast a whole range of problems in a myriad of formulations that all had the common feature of uniting corporations and workers against a "new class" of radicalized professionals and academics in league with a dangerous "underclass."[35]

Conservatives did not have a monopoly on such attitudes. Plenty of liberal politicians eagerly embraced the tough-on-crime rhetoric of the 1980s, as did many middle-class African Americans worried about the apparent breakdown of their communities.[36] But the demand for a crackdown was more persuasively and persistently woven into conservative ideology, where it appeared not like a bolted-on addition, but a natural extension of first principles.

US, THEM, AND GOVERNMENT

As conservatives incorporated libertarians into the broad ideological tent that *National Review* founder Frank Meyer called fusionism, they absorbed the doctrine that government is inherently self-interested and expansionary, a captive of special interests rather than a servant of the public interest.[37] Academic libertarians modeled this belief under the title of "public-choice theory."[38] In a less formal way it became part of the folk theory of the conservative grass roots.

Public-sector unions, for instance, needed to be weakened because they reduced the flexibility of government, obstructed effective management, and drove up the cost of personnel. The only way to get control over agencies that had become captured by special interests was to impose strong "outcome" measures, quantifiable benchmarks that would substitute for the lack of market discipline. Exhibit A for these arguments was public schools: Conservatives and some New Democrats lamented the power of teachers' unions and insisted on holding educators responsible for the performance of their students, as measured by test scores.[39]

Where criminal justice was concerned, however, these arguments were roundly ignored. Schools, social welfare, and housing were all fair game for the claim of being out of control, since they helped those whom conservatives viewed as "takers." But conservatives were vigorously in favor of expanding the parts of government that they sympathized with, those they associated with the "makers" and forces of order.[40]

From the vantage point of working politicians and their voters, as opposed to conservative intellectuals, conservatism was mainly about the maintenance of order, rather than resistance to the state. In this battle, law enforcement represented the "good guys." Thus, Reagan told a group of police chiefs in 1981 they were "the thin blue line that holds back a jungle which threatens to reclaim this clearing we call civilization." Meanwhile, the metaphor of a war on crime made police and prisons the domestic equivalents of the U.S. military in its struggle against Communist forces. As Reagan Attorney General William French put it, "The Justice Department is not a domestic agency. It is the internal arm of the national defense."[41] Law-enforcement professionals could turn back the tide of violence, but only if politicians gave them the resources and authority they needed, instead of second-guessing them or fettering them with more rules.

In fact, conservative arguments about the criminal justice system paralleled those they made about the misbegotten civilian meddling with the military they blamed for the nation's failure in Vietnam. The profession of Arms, whether in green or blue, was a violent business. When those of tender, liberal sensibilities shrank from this truth, the enemy was emboldened. The 1992 Republican Platform linked the causes of law enforcement and national defense, declaring: "We believe in giving police the resources to do their job . . . We have led efforts to increase the number of police protecting our citizens. We also support incentives to encourage personnel leaving the Armed Forces to continue to defend their country—against the enemy within—by entering the law enforcement profession."[42] Thus, conservatives assiduously avoided tarring prison guard unions with the same brush they applied to teachers' unions, or imposing on criminal justice anything like the audit regime they imposed on public schools.[43] Victims were given a similarly privileged status, as those paying the price for a society unwilling to stand up to civilizational decline.

Victims' groups and law enforcement were never part of the Republican coalition in the sense that they wielded the electoral or financial muscle to have a seat at the party table with gun owners, business, or the religious right. But their cultural status in conservative ideology demanded deference to their concerns. Thus, conservatives of this era did not want to shrink the state across the board. They wanted to shrink those parts of it they associated with the forces of disorder and the professionals who served them.

So, conservatives took the side of cops against liberal innovations such as civilian review boards and the criminal procedure revolution symbolized by the Supreme Court's *Miranda* decision. While liberals increasingly worried about the conditions in prisons and litigated to change them, conservatives argued that prisons were difficult places because criminals were dangerous, and that court-ordered prison reforms had the impact of shackling the authority of guards and making lock-ups harder to govern.[44] And of course, conservatives argued that criminal sentences were much too low to be an effective deterrent to crime, or to incapacitate genuinely dangerous men.

Conservatives were especially hostile to efforts at rehabilitation, which were seen as importing the mindset and personnel of the bad, social service side of government into the hard, no-nonsense side of criminal justice. Worse than the fact that none of the measures proposed by liberals had actually put a dent in crime, conservatives argued that rehabilitative measures reflected excessive sympathy for criminals.[45] Rather than innocent victims of society deserving of the services of a generous welfare state, criminals were better characterized as constitutionally malevolent victimizers of the innocent.

What worked, conservatives said simply, were long sentences, which would keep those behind bars from preying on society and send a message to those outside that severe retribution awaited them if they violated society's laws.[46] Liberals were, in this argument, insufficiently "pro-government" when its operatives were cops, prosecutors, and prison guards. Public choice analysis stopped at the prison door.

Reflecting on his philosophy at the time, Nolan turns to Isaiah 32:18: "My people will live in peaceful communities, in secure homes, and in tranquil places of rest."[47] "And that's just a beautiful picture," Nolan says. "And I then extended that—therefore we need to lock up more people, because if we got the bad guys off the street, then we would have peace, security and tranquility. It was a kind of straight-line logic that animated what I did."[48]

But for both Nolan and the conservative movement he helped to build, the straight line from fighting crime to building prisons would eventually take a sharp turn.

CHAPTER 3

Cracks in the Wall

Julie Stewart took on a lonely battle when she founded Families Against Mandatory Minimums in 1991. Stewart left a good job as public-affairs director at the libertarian Cato Foundation to start a nonprofit with uncertain finances and an almost hopeless cause. But she had a deeply personal reason to take the risk. Stewart's brother, Jeff, had just been sentenced to five years in federal prison for growing marijuana in the garage of his home in Washington State. Jeff had been betrayed by two accomplices, who got off with probation in exchange for turning him in. It was Jeff's first brush with the law, and his judge said the sentence was unfair, but he had no choice under federal statutes mandating minimum sentences for drug offenses.[1] While Stewart's libertarian background had always made her skeptical of the nation's drug laws, the increasingly common injustice meted out to Jeff propelled her to lobby to keep the same thing from happening to other people's loved ones.

Cato had long been a lonely outpost of resistance to the drug war, which was one of the key issues where libertarians distinguished themselves from, and were ignored by, their

Republican allies. Stewart's new organization did score an early victory in 1994 when it helped persuade Congress to create a small statutory window for some drug offenders to escape the full weight of the federal mandatory minimums.[2] But for the most part, she and her libertarian friends were shouting into the wilderness, viewed by mainstream Republicans as one step removed from the readers of *High Times*. Conservatives put up with libertarians' views on drug policy because they were so useful on matters like economic regulation, but those positions were seen as an eccentricity, not a wake-up call.[3] Religious conservatives such as Chuck Colson, whom we discuss in detail in chapter 4, and the evangelical Harvard Law Professor William Stuntz, who very publicly criticized the expansion of prosecutors' power and the differential impact of the war on drugs, were just as roundly ignored in Congress and state legislatures.[4]

"I didn't think it would be so hard," Stewart reflected in 2012. "I didn't know I'd be here 21 years later."[5]

No matter how smart and persuasive they were, people such as Colson, Stuntz, and Stewart would make little headway until their audience in the Republican Party changed. For many years, conservatives took tough-on-crime positions because they made electoral sense, and no amount of crafty persuasion was going to get them to change until that stopped working. Personal networks, identity vouching, and increasingly sophisticated organizations were necessary to change the way conservatives thought about crime; but first the structural ground upon which partisan support for mass incarceration rested had to shift. *Fortuna* had to turn their way.

WHEN CRIME NO LONGER PAYS

For decades, getting tough on crime was seen by working politicians as an essential ingredient in electoral success, but by the late 2000s, the issue had lost much of its kick. Three trends are primarily responsible. First, success spawned imitation, as Democrats made a concerted effort to break the GOP's monopoly on the crime issue during the Clinton era. Second, crime itself began dropping precipitously during the 1990s—a change that ultimately resulted in a less-jittery public. Third, the intrusion of terrorism displaced crime as Americans' top security concern.

As Figure 3-1 shows, the public tended to trust the GOP more than the Democrats on issues of drugs and law and order, with occasional exceptions, through the 1980s. But the "New Democrats" of the Clinton era made a concerted effort to stop offering their chin. As David Holian argues,

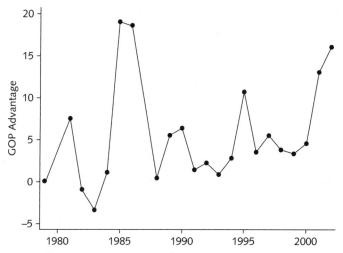

Figure 3-1 GOP Advantage on Law and Order Issues, 1979–2002.
Source: Jeremy C. Pope and Jonathan Woon, "Measuring Changes in American Party Reputations, 1939–2004," *Political Research Quarterly* 62, no. 4 (December 2009): 653–61. GOP advantage represents the difference between percentages of survey respondents who express a preference for Republicans and those who express a preference for Democrats on questions of law and order.

Bill Clinton adopted a "Yes, but" reply to the GOP, accepting key premises of the Republican platform but adding the new angle of prevention through expanded policing and gun control. The effects were impressive. In 1996, more voters said they trusted Clinton to handle crime than Bob Dole, his Republican rival.[6] In 1999, *Campaigns and Elections* magazine observed that Republicans were counting on their signature issues, "from attacking moral breakdown to continuing a welfare overhaul, from fiscal responsibility to crime control," to carry them in the following year's elections. "The bitter irony for conservatives," the magazine continued, "is that their success in moving the nation toward their side on many of these issues has taken them away as prime campaign fodder—at least for now."[7] As Republican office seekers and their consultants got the message that voters no longer thought their party owned the crime issue, it made sense to switch their attention to issues on which they still had an advantage.

Meanwhile, rates of violent crime began to nosedive in the mid-1990s. The crime drop appears to have begun registering with the mass public by the latter years of the 1990s, as smaller proportions of Americans began identifying crime-related problems as the nation's most pressing issue in Gallup surveys.[8] As Figure 3-2 shows, crime-related issues have now nearly disappeared from the public's consciousness.

With voters no longer as agitated by crime as they once were, and with party positions no longer as distinct, politicians' interest in the issue went through the floor. Data from the Policy Agendas Project shows that across the political system, attention to crime dropped sharply after the mid-1990s. Congressional hearings on crime, for example, peaked in 1996 and plummeted by 2002 when terrorism is excluded (Figure 3-3).

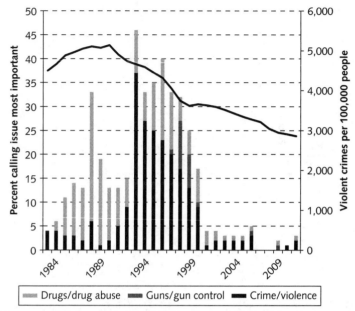

Figure 3-2 Violent Crime and "Most Important Problem"
Responses, 1984–2012.
Source: "Table 2.1.2012, Attitudes Toward the Most Important Problem
Facing the Country" (Sourcebook of Criminal Justice Statistics Online),
http://www.albany.edu/sourcebook/pdf/t212012.pdf.

The decline in both public and policymaker attention
to crime was reinforced by the intrusion of the terrorism
issue. After the attacks of September 11, 2001, counter-
terrorism dominated public discussion of law enforcement. As Figure 3-3 shows, terrorism accounted for the
vast majority of hearings coded in the "crime" category
of the Policy Agendas Project in the 2001–2005 period.
Politicians who just a few years earlier would have pur-
sued more pedestrian cops-and-robbers issues were now
focused on the new threat, limiting their capacity to take

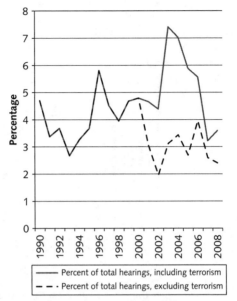

Figure 3-3 Percent of Congressional Hearings on Crime, with and without Terrorism, 1990–2008.
Source: Policy Agendas Project, "Congressional Hearings Dataset" (University of Texas at Austin, n.d.), http:// www.policyagendas.org/ page/ datasets- codebooks#congressional_ hear.

up the traditional law-and-order cause. And while Figure 3-1 shows that the Republican advantage on law and order bumped back up in the aftermath of 9/11, it did so in the context of a drastically lower level of issue salience than its previous heights in the 1980s. Voters once again trusted Republicans more on crime, but now they simply did not care about it very much. Republicans responded rationally by shifting their attention to terrorism, which voters most certainly *did* care about.

Ironically, the importance of the crime issue also shrank because Republican power expanded at the state level. Since at least the 1960s, the GOP had been converting conservative Democrats to its side by stressing social issues, especially crime.[9] By the mid-2000s, however, this long process of partisan conversion was almost complete.[10] With the GOP's dominance in conservative states assured, the electoral value of wedge issues like crime declined. What is more, Republicans now owned responsibility, including fiscal responsibility, for state government. Paradoxically, then, it was in these most conservative states that Republicans had the most leeway to rethink their attachment to tough-on-crime positions, and the most reason to actually change them.

The result of these changes was to slow the self-replicating dynamics in which initial success with "tough-on-crime" politics encouraged more politicians to pile on. Instead, the opposite dynamic took hold, as the withdrawal of attention to crime by some politicians encouraged others to pull back as well.

BIG GOVERNMENT IS EVERYWHERE

Along with shifts in the politics of crime itself, the other crucial impetus for reframing incarceration in terms of efficiency and cost has been the rightward ideological shift in the conservative movement. The more the party deepens its hostility to government, the less willing Republican office holders are to give prisons an exemption from their critique of government as inefficient, unjust, inherently expansionary, and unaccountable. Ironically, conservatives have become more likely to agree with liberals on crime for precisely the same reason that they are more likely to disagree on just about everything else. And this increasing anti-statism on issues such as criminal justice appeared earlier and with greater potency at the state level, where legislative turnover is higher than in Congress, and where consequently fewer members have well-established views that they would need to reverse.[11]

Many observers who attribute the newfound interest in sentencing reform primarily to economic pressures have missed this underlying ideological shift. To be sure, the aftermath of the 2001 recession coincided with an initial round of reform, and the deeper downturn after 2008 has seen a more sweeping round of changes.[12] In every state that has passed sentencing reforms, saving money has been invoked as a major justification. The pressure prisons are putting on state budgets also helps to explain why, in many states, business leaders have become cheerleaders for prison reform.[13]

The economic account is seriously incomplete, however. Both history and theory suggest economic downturns can be associated with significant growth of the correctional apparatus, rather than the opposite.[14] As Figure 3-4 shows, prison costs rose sharply in the 1980s and 1990s. The claim that these expenses were unsustainable was in fact being

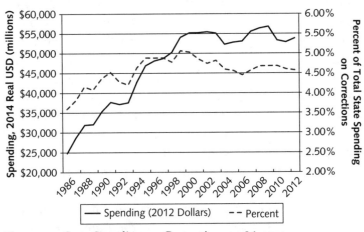

Figure 3-4 State Spending on Corrections, 1986–2012.
Source: National Association of State Budget Officers.

made in these decades, including by some conservatives, but it fell on deaf ears.[15] A budget-driven account also fails to explain the timing of recent developments. Prison populations began to change during the strong part of the economic cycle, in 2007. As the Pew Charitable Trusts notes, "Total state admissions to prison declined in 2007, well before the economic collapse, and again in 2008."[16] As a symbolic matter, too, practitioners date the turning point for reforms to 2007. As we discuss in chapter 6, that was the year that Texas, one of the nation's top jailers per capita, passed a sweeping sentencing reform package even though the state was basking in a surplus that allowed the legislature to hike overall spending by 10 percent over the previous year.[17]

Corrections have not become too expensive in some objective sense. Instead, Tea Party–inspired Republicans, by creating a climate of permanent austerity in the states that they control, made the GOP's longtime exemption for police and prisons ideologically and fiscally untenable. This is not a purely cyclical, budgetary phenomenon, one that would disappear with the next upswing. It is a politically generated, secular shift in the trajectory of Republican politics on criminal justice. Self-inflicted austerity and the rise of a more radically anti-statist mood in the Republican Party provided an opening for criminal-justice reformers, who believed in change for their own reasons, to get the ear of Republicans who were not willing to listen before.[18]

A SHIFTED PLAYING FIELD

These structural changes, taken together, have altered the electoral appeal of criminal justice for practical politicians. From the 1970s to the 1990s, crime, public fear, media attention, and political rhetoric mutually reinforced one another. As crime rates went up, the public expressed greater fear of crime, which led the media to cover it more intensely and politicians to appeal to voters promising to do something about it. The frenzied rhetoric generated even greater public fear, leading to still more media and political attention.

The decline of crime has broken this self-reinforcing cycle and possibly created a downward cascade in its stead. With crime rates dropping, the public's fear subsided, and the media and politicians reduced the degree to which they reinforced that fear. In addition, politicians who oversaw large decreases in crime had every incentive to let their voters know that crime had actually gone down. That then led to even lower public fear, and even less attention. And of course, in the aftermath of the September 11 attacks, Americans had something much more frightening than street crime to worry about, and for politicians to compete on.

Meanwhile, the GOP itself was changing. A new generation of conservatives inherited their elders' hostility to government and purified it. Not raised in the crucible of the crime wars, they were open to seeing prisons as just another part of big government—an armed welfare state. Those same conservatives were also imposing increasingly strict fiscal discipline on states they controlled. That made it harder and harder to exempt the corrections budget from the same scrutiny they were placing on traditional objects of their ire such as social services.

These changes meant that conservatives determined to change their movement's positions on criminal justice were no longer battling uphill. They did not have to ask Republicans to give up an issue that was working for them, or push against the grain of what the party was saying in other areas. As early as 2001, the combination of these political changes with recessionary budget pressure began to show effects, as several states launched modest experiments to slow the growth of their prison systems.[19] Still, these structural changes did not make the decline of tough-on-crime thinking inevitable. The movement would need a lot of persuasion to break with old ideas and inherited reputations.

CHAPTER 4

Rounding Up a Posse

While the brunt of America's war on crime fell on the nation's most disadvantaged citizens, the prison explosion did not leave the nation's governing elite unscathed. Some were ensnared directly in the web, while others saw family members pulled in. Unlike high school dropouts, these people had the connections and political savvy to fight back.[1] Julie Stewart was one of them.

Pat Nolan was another.

In 1986, the FBI office in Sacramento began investigating corruption in the California legislature.[2] To test its theory that some legislators were on the take, the agency invented a company, "Peach State Capital," that wanted to open a shrimp-processing plant in California. Agents persuaded a legislator to file a bill that would help Peach State build the imaginary plant. The feds apparently made a compelling case for the shellfish industry, because the bill passed the Assembly by an overwhelming majority that included Nolan. Perhaps surprised by its own lobbying prowess, the FBI had to warn Gov. George Deukmejian that the legislation was merely a charade; he vetoed the bill but kept the secret, allowing agents posing as Peach State's "executives" to keep working the capitol.[3]

In the next round of FBI lobbying, the agency alleged, Nolan promised to help "Peach State Capital" with its bill as a quid pro quo for a $10,000 campaign donation. In fact, agents had left the recipient's name blank on the check they handed to Nolan, opening the door for him to cash it in his personal account and implicate himself in outright bribery. Instead, he divided the money between political committees and reported it as a campaign contribution. The story broke in 1988, but no charges were filed. Five years later, the U.S. attorney had Nolan indicted on six counts related to the FBI investigation, just before the statute of limitations was to expire.[4] Facing at least eight years in prison if convicted on a single charge, Nolan decided to accept a plea bargain in which he was sentenced to 33 months.[5] On April 4, 1994, he reported to the federal prison camp at Dublin, California, far from his family in Southern California, to begin serving his sentence.[6]

On his first night, Nolan's bed had no sheets or pillow. Other inmates gave him bedding and made him some ramen soup. The reception from his fellow prisoners was a pleasant surprise, but there were many bitter lessons to follow. Nolan soon realized that much of what he had believed about prisons was wrong. Drugs were plentiful, but rehabilitation programming was not. Harassment by the guards was routine. "Who do you think you are?," Nolan recalls a staffer yelling at him. "You're worthless. You're nothing." To this day, Nolan chokes up when he talks about the impact of his absence on his wife and children.[7]

The family found some solace, however, through a connection to Prison Fellowship, an evangelical organization that ministers to inmates and their families. Prison Fellowship was led by Charles Colson, a former aide to

President Richard Nixon who became infamous in the Watergate scandal. In the midst of the crisis, Colson had a born-again experience, and after serving out a prison term for his misdeeds in the White House, he founded Prison Fellowship to help others turn away from crime.

At an awards ceremony honoring Nolan in absentia, a friend introduced Nolan's wife to Colson. Following that meeting, the Nolans enrolled their kids in a Prison Fellowship program for children of inmates and Pat began talking regularly with Colson. Even before Nolan's release, Colson offered him a job running Prison Fellowship's policy arm, Justice Fellowship, which had been languishing. Nolan jumped at the chance. "I'd really been praying about 'Okay, Lord, what's the next chapter in my life?'" Nolan recalled. "I'd seen so much injustice while I was inside that I felt I really wanted to address that. My eyes had been opened."[8]

Nolan would spend the rest of his life trying to open the eyes of his fellow conservatives. The core building blocks for this work were the reputations and relationships that he and Colson had built up over the years. Colson was a towering figure in evangelical circles, and his near-mythological status had already begun to generate some mass appeal for the cause of redeeming prisoners. Nolan did not share his boss's fame, but his own history as a crime warrior and conservative leader in California made him impossible to dismiss as a closet liberal. When Colson and Nolan talked, other figures in the movement had to listen.

Their reputation came bundled with another asset— relationships. Colson and Nolan enjoyed the trust of key leaders in the conservative movement and considered many of them friends. Those friends were willing to hear their arguments sympathetically, give them strategic advice, and loan their own reputations to the cause by signing letters and making contact with others who might be helpful. Once these conservative leaders pitched in, even in a small way, they often became drawn into increasingly deep engagement with the cause.

Out of these gradual conversions to rethinking corrections, Colson and Nolan were able to form a genuine reform cadre, one with power at the highest levels of the Republican Party. Leveraging this cadre's connections and political savvy, Colson and Nolan very carefully chose legislation designed to appeal to conservatives, experimented with ways to fuse different strands of conservative and libertarian ideas to justify reform, and relentlessly pushed their cause to create a sense of urgency and mission. Many of their investments of time, resources, and networks would not pan out for years, often in ways that they never predicted. But all of them were aimed at the same target: opening conservatives' eyes to the pathologies of the criminal justice system and making concern with the degradation of prisoners a legitimately conservative cause.

THE MAN WHO MADE REFORM CONSERVATIVE

In 2014, Congress created a task force to study ways to reduce the number of federal prisoners. Tellingly, Congress named that task force after someone who never ran for political office and never ran a prison. In fact, they named it after a convicted felon. The Charles Colson Task Force on Federal Corrections was nonetheless aptly named, for it was Colson who, almost single-handedly, made sympathy and concern for the welfare of criminals legitimate in conservative circles. His fingerprints continue to be all over the modern reform cause.

Colson opened one of his many books by relating President Nixon's reaction to the prison riot in Attica, New York, in 1971. Governor Nelson Rockefeller had ordered police to raid the prison, resulting in a bloodbath.[9] Colson recalls that Nixon was impressed with Rockefeller's response: "Rockefeller did the right thing, Chuck . . . He'll catch it though from all those liberal jackasses in the press. But he's smart. The public want no nonsense from criminals. The public will cheer him on. 'Gun 'em down,' they'll say."[10] Colson wrote up a note to his staff, making clear that they "must get tough . . . It was good politics. We believed that long sentences, increased police powers and tough prisons were the answer to the crime problem."[11]

"Neither of us mentioned the 31 prisoners who had been killed," Colson recalled, "but I suggested that the President send personal letters to the families of the nine slain guards. A nice gesture."[12] To be a conservative was to have one's sympathies in the right place, with the defenders of order. Convicted criminals were hardly worthy of similar concern.

Watergate broke less than a year later. Colson was among the high-level Nixon aides who were ultimately indicted for their role in the scandal. As Colson explained in his best-selling book, *Born Again*, Watergate was a shattering, transformative experience for him, leading him to examine his sins and devote himself to God.[13] Colson later pled guilty to a charge of obstruction of justice and served seven months in prison. His own conversion gave Colson the certainty that no one was beyond redemption. After he served his time, the white-hot faith forged in the crucible of Watergate led Colson back into prisons across the nation, where he was resolved to do the Lord's work. Colson was convinced that this project was important not just to the inmates, but also to those who ministered to them. Christian faith, he believed, was weak and inauthentic if not tested by a real human relationship to the "least of these."

Over time, Prison Fellowship blossomed. It reaches some 200,000 inmates annually, spread over more than 1,400 lockups in all 50 states.[14] Hundreds of thousands of children of inmates receive presents each Christmas through a Prison Fellowship program.[15] Suffusing all its activities is a genuine—and at times very controversial—religious fellowship. Glenn Loury, a Brown University economist who served on the Prison Fellowship board for five years, recalls that board meetings always began with worship. "They had a literal ceremony," Loury said. "They had preaching and music, and singing, and prayer, and my first meeting, I was invited to give my testimony, which is to say, to tell the story of how I became a Christian, which I was happy to do."[16] To join the leadership of Prison Fellowship, potential board members had to demonstrate that their faith was solid. Loury recalls that, before he joined, he went through "an inquisition. I had to sit down with the chief theological [officer]. He asked me about salvation. He asked me what did I think Jesus was about. I can't remember all the questions, but they were probing, and there were correct and incorrect answers."[17] The Christianity that Colson advocated was of a deeply humbling sort. Loury believes that for Colson's volunteers, prison visits had the function of making "real this idea that Christ was crucified next to a common thief, who achieved salvation and eternal life, because even at the last minute, he was prepared to affirm and believe, and follow the Lord. And this forgiveness, this idea that, whatever the transgression, there's a possibility of redemption."[18]

Colson defined evangelical theological orthodoxy and the Christian vocation for more than three decades. Unlike the Catholic Church, evangelical denominations have no hierarchy to define legitimate leadership, nothing other than a reputation for godliness recognized by others of the faith—and Colson had as much of that as any other evangelical leader in his generation. After his death, he was celebrated by Christian Coalition founder Ralph Reed as among "the most influential evangelical leaders of the last half-century" and by Focus on the Family President Jim Daly as "one of the great modern-day lions of the faith."[19]

As real as Colson's religious vision was, however, what distinguished him was his hybrid role as a spiritual leader and hardball political strategist. University of Pennsylvania political scientist John DiIulio, another Prison Fellowship board member and a close Colson confidant, argues that where the conservative criminal justice community is concerned, "I don't think anything much happened without Chuck being apprised and engaged ... You know, they say that Karl Rove is a brilliant strategist, but I don't think anybody ever lived that was better at that stuff than Chuck Colson."[20] Loury supports DiIulio's recollection, noting, "He was a rock-ribbed conservative ... He was still Chuck Colson, after he got to work again. He was an operative. He was Bill Kristol on steroids."[21] Former U.S. Congressman Frank Wolf, another close friend of Colson's, said, "There has not been a person who has filled the role of Colson. You get religious leaders who come at it from a religious perspective. You get political leaders who come at it maybe from a different perspective. Chuck combined those two together in a very, very unique way. When Chuck Colson spoke, generally the faith community as well as the political community listened."[22]

Colson's credibility as a political strategist on criminal justice was enhanced by his orthodox positions on other issues. Colson was one of the nation's most recognized opponents of abortion, and he took deeply conservative positions on issues such as homosexuality, feminism, and euthanasia. His opposition to Supreme Court decisions on such questions was so strident that he said Christians should seriously consider "some kind of direct, extra-political confrontation of the judicially controlled regime."[23]

That reputation for orthodoxy was a powerful political tool, allowing Colson to break with the conservative line in the 1980s and 1990s, when his vision on criminal justice was still very far from the Republican mainstream. DiIulio recalls that "There was a sense in which ... we're taking the long view. It's going to take a while for this to mushroom, and for people to come aboard."[24] In a time when significant legislative victories seemed nearly impossible, Colson focused on "planting these mustard seeds ... [The growth of prisons] didn't happen overnight, and it's not going to be addressed, or it's not going to be resolved, overnight."[25]

Among Colson's mustard seeds was the influence he had on people who would go on to be major figures in the conservative movement, many of whom became key allies in criminal-justice reform. Among the most prominent is Michael Gerson, President George W. Bush's chief speechwriter and now a columnist at the *Washington Post*. Gerson worked for Colson for three years immediately after graduating from Wheaton College. He claims that Colson was, after his family, "the single most influential person in my life."[26]

Another example is Colson's friendship with Frank Wolf (who as a congressional appropriator became an important supporter of funding for state-level reforms, among his other contributions to the cause). One of Wolf's daughters married a top Colson deputy at Prison Fellowship, and Wolf's son worked for Colson. "He was a big influence on me," Wolf said.[27] Gerson and Wolf were not the only members of the Washington elite who saw Colson as a spiritual leader. In 2005, Colson gave a lecture series based on his book *How Now Shall We Live* to members of Congress.[28] Lawmakers also read tributes into the *Congressional Record* after his death. Indiana Senator Dan Coats called Colson a "friend, confidant, and mentor."[29] Rep. Steve King of Iowa declared, "We are dazzled by the life of Chuck Colson."[30]

Beyond the Beltway, two of the most important conservative donors to the cause were directly recruited by Chuck Colson. Tim Dunn, whose philanthropy will be discussed in chapter 7, became interested in criminal justice through listening to Colson's radio program.[31] Meanwhile, Colson personally signed up B. Wayne Hughes, a major Republican donor, as a Prison Fellowship supporter at a Ronald Reagan Presidential Library event in 2009.[32] In 2014, Hughes put his financial weight behind California's Proposition 47, which reduced penalties for minor drug and property crimes and directed the savings into correctional services. Tellingly, Hughes denies that the fiscal costs of mass incarceration were behind his engagement with the issue: "At the end of the day, for me it's a matter of the heart. You can look at the economics, but it's only because I went to prison [to visit inmates] and saw the fallout of over-incarceration that I realized we can't just keep doing the same thing."[33]

Colson planted mustard seeds well beyond the elites of politics and business, too. Just as important were the thousands of rank-and-file evangelicals whom he drew into prisons, who slowly but surely convinced other conservative Christians that prisoners were appropriate objects of personal compassion, and that criminal justice was a legitimate object of their political engagement. As Richard Land of the Southern Baptist Convention explains, "When evangelicals became aware, largely through Chuck Colson's ministry, in a grassroots way [of] the abuses that were going on in prison, they were upset about it and they wanted to do something about it. And they certainly wanted to defend their right to have Bible studies ... As they themselves got involved with prisoners and their families it put a human face on it and from that they became more sensitive to the issues and to the abuses."[34]

Suggestive qualitative research with conservative Christians engaged in prison ministry shows that they are, in fact, much more likely to embrace a framework of compassion than their larger community, which is characterized by a disproportionately punitive approach to law and order.[35] As one of the sources the researchers spoke to put it,

> So often we have an attitude that people in prison are there because they deserve to be, which is a very harsh mindset. While I do not debate the fact that people have to be punished for the mistakes they make, I think it gave me a greater sensitivity that they are still people. When you actually get to sit down and talk to people and put a name with a face and realize that this person has a family, a baby, and wife, you actually start to see them as people and not just a prisoner or a number.[36]

As more conservative Christians engaged in prison ministry, led by Colson and Prison Fellowship, they became ambassadors who could share this compassionate framework with their fellow parishioners.

Colson also played a major role in expanding the vision of Prison Fellowship from saving individual souls to considering the collateral impact on the families of prisoners, which would become a major theme in convincing social conservatives of the harm of mass incarceration. DiIulio recalls that this wider vision grew out of the "Angel Tree" program, which gives Christmas presents to the children of inmates. "This was a major shift in the paradigm of Chuck's thinking, which I kept talking about. CYF, CYF, CYF: children, youth, and families of prisoners and those affected by crime... This basically opens the doors to all of the negative consequences of incarceration, and that becomes a legitimate thing to talk about, and even to do ministry around as part of prison ministry."[37] It also got the attention of socially conservative organizations focused on family issues, such as the Faith and Freedom Coalition, American Values, and the Family Research Council, Nolan said. "What it did was open their eyes to impact beyond just the inmate, that really there are consequences and there are victims of crime that aren't thought of usually," Nolan said.[38]

FROM SYMPATHY TO ACTION

Colson had started the policy arm of Prison Fellowship, dubbed Justice Fellowship, in 1983 after a shocking visit to a Washington State prison where many inmates were held in solitary confinement.[39] Despite the long-term investments Colson was making in changing minds, however, the policy unit did not win much notoriety until Nolan took the helm. "Until Pat showed up and took it, I'd never even heard of the Justice Fellowship," said FAMM's Julie Stewart. "Pat is really responsible for the evangelical attention to why are we putting so many people in prison in the first place, or at least for so long."[40] From the start, Nolan's assignment was ambitious—abolishing mandatory minimum sentences across the board, improving prison conditions, and, as Nolan puts it, "reducing the reliance on incarceration" in general.[41]

Nolan soon realized that he could only make progress by winning over conservatives. Traumatized liberals were unlikely to take on reform without solid cover from the right. Meanwhile, the handful of conservatives who were open to the cause could not sustain themselves without some help from inside their camp.[42]

Nolan was not the only criminal-justice activist looking for conservative allies. Around the time he joined Prison Fellowship, a liberal congressional staffer named Virginia Sloan was growing increasingly concerned about efforts to chip away at the right of death-row inmates to file so-called habeas corpus appeals in federal courts. Sloan founded an "Emergency Committee to Save Habeas Corpus," chaired by four former attorneys general—two Democrats and two Republicans. She soon left Capitol Hill to found the Constitution Project, a nonprofit focused on developing such bipartisan coalitions on constitutional issues.[43] Sloan and Nolan began a productive collaboration. "Whatever issue we work on, whether it's a formal relationship or not, we're always on the phone with Pat. Because he's so smart and so strategic and we can help him think about ways to look at things and he helps us think about ways to look at things," Sloan said.[44]

Nolan and Sloan both found a crucial supporter in David Keene, who at the time was president of the American Conservative Union, the organization that hosts the annual Conservative Political Action Conference. He would go on to become president of the National Rifle Association and an editor at the *Washington Times*. A veteran of Goldwater's Young Americans for Freedom, Keene was an old friend of Nolan's. He had also known Colson for decades, going back to the days when Keene was an assistant to Nixon's vice president, Spiro Agnew. Keene began working with the Constitution Project at the turn of the millennium. He would go on to lead one of its civil-liberties committees following the September 11, 2001, attacks and also became a regular consultant on the death penalty and broader criminal-justice issues.

Keene had long been interested in crime policy, partly as an offshoot of his involvement with the gun-rights cause, and believed that conservatives had gone astray on the issue. Keene traces the start of the problem to a liberal philosophy that always sought to absolve the criminal. That, he said, led to the issue being framed in polarizing terms. "You either supported the cops or the criminals, and that was the juxtaposition," he said, adding that when liberals made excuses for criminals, "the conservatives fell into that by saying, 'Well, no, the answer is to lock them all up.'" To escape these poles, Keene said, "you have to start by saying the number one goal—and this is what we preach to the conservatives—the number one goal is a safer society and a civilized society where people can walk the streets and live in their communities."[45]

In 1999, Keene spoke out for reforming the civil asset-forfeiture laws that allow police to confiscate property from people never convicted of a crime.[46] He also penned an op-ed lamenting conservatives' failure to resist expansions to wiretapping rights under the Clinton administration and other such "threats posing as tools needed by law enforcement in the nation's continuing war on crime. There is, in fact, an incredibly naive tendency on the right to assume that laws directed at 'criminals' aren't a threat to the rest of us," Keene wrote.[47]

This type of ideological analysis and innovation was exactly what Sloan was looking for when she started the Constitution Project. The idea was not to develop positions that represented ideological compromise. Rather, it was to find conservatives who agreed with Sloan and other liberals for their own reasons. "It really wasn't until the Emergency Committee to Save Habeas that for the first time, we reached out to people who don't think like us," Sloan said. "Those were people who could open doors that liberals couldn't open. They could make arguments in language that liberals couldn't do, or people wouldn't listen to them. But if . . . Dave Keene could call up somebody, it's going to be very different from some prominent liberal. And he might make a different kind of argument, or in a different way, but he gets to the same place."[48]

Another early recruit to Nolan's reform cadre was Richard Viguerie, who helped form the "New Right" in the 1970s through his pioneering use of direct mail on behalf of conservative causes. A fellow Catholic and veteran of Young Americans for Freedom, Viguerie was already an active opponent of the death penalty. It was Viguerie who had introduced Nolan's wife to Colson while Nolan was incarcerated. Viguerie said his interest in criminal justice was enhanced when people he knew went to prison for what he considered excessive terms.[49]

Both Keene and Viguerie were sympathetic to the broader cause of criminal-justice reform, but it took Nolan to get them to act on those sympathies, Keene said:

> We all took individual positions, and Richard Viguerie and I were concerned about doing something—but we hadn't done very much. As Viguerie likes to tell you, to succeed at anything and to raise any issue you really need a champion, a driver, and that's the role that Pat Nolan played in all this. Gathering people that shared the concerns was not overly difficult. Getting them to actually take that concern and begin to transform it into public

action is a different story. It required someone to say "Let's
do this," or, "We can do something."[50]

In the early years, Nolan would talk with Keene and
Viguerie on an ad hoc basis to discuss strategy on Prison
Fellowship's legislative priorities, including efforts to safeguard prisoners' religious rights. "They were a great sound-
ing board to [which] arguments were the strongest, what
would be the most convincing to conservatives," Nolan
said.[51]

Keene's commitment to the cause soon became intensely
personal. In 2002, his 21-year-old son was sentenced to
10 years in federal prison for firing a gun during a road-rage
incident, despite a history of mental illness.[52] In Keene's
telling, a hard-charging federal prosecutor threatened to
pile on charges if his son rejected a plea deal. The difficul-
ties Keene said his son went through in prison—struggling
for access to medicine, suffering harassment by guards,
being transferred to a tougher facility out of spite—only
further sensitized the conservative leader to the reality of
life behind bars.

Nolan and Colson had another close ally in Edwin Meese,
who served as one of Ronald Reagan's top White House
advisors before becoming his attorney general. Meese had
known both men for many years—in fact, the first fateful
meeting between Colson and Nolan's wife occurred at an
event where the Council for National Policy, a conservative group then led by Meese, was giving Nolan an award
in absentia. Based at the Heritage Foundation, Meese was
pursuing his own agenda of bipartisan outreach on justice issues, focused on what Meese and other critics called
"over-criminalization." Their concern was twofold: that
the federal government was seizing criminal jurisdiction

in matters best left to the states, and that criminal law was becoming so pervasive that even conduct most people would consider trivial could result in a prison sentence. In discussing the federalization phenomenon, over-criminalization critics tended to emphasize needless federal jurisdiction over street crime.[53] The conservative concern with ever-broadening law, meanwhile, stressed white-collar and regulatory offenses. Both tracks eventually opened up space for conservatives to cast the drug war as simply another version of the same government overreach that criminalized lobster importers, grandmothers who failed to trim their hedges, and snowmobilers who drifted onto federal land in a blizzard.[54]

Meese was remarkably early in considering the excesses of the nation's campaign against crime. He worked with Nolan in 1998 to arrange a meeting with a small group of conservative members of Congress, including 1980s crime warrior Dan Lungren, to discuss reform of mandatory-minimum sentencing.[55] Meese also visited a Prison Fellowship program in Texas to learn more about the organization's approach to rehabilitation and reentry.[56] He advocated for expanded use of compassionate release for inmates in 1999.[57] Several years later, Meese would also work with the Constitution Project on mapping a path forward after the U.S. Supreme Court upended the Reagan-era system of federal sentencing guidelines.[58]

Colson and Nolan also tapped their contacts in the community of religious conservatives, calling on such organizations as the National Association of Evangelicals, Southern Baptist Convention, and Family Research Council to endorse their evolving legislative agenda, which will be described in chapter 9. In a reflection of the deference Prison Fellowship commands, Galen Carey of the National Association of Evangelicals said, "They are a well-respected organization among almost all our constituents. They have expertise in, specialization in this area that we don't have—people on the staff who are just prison experts. Whenever we are considering things, I talk to Pat or someone else over there."[59] The Southern Baptists' Land put this conversion of reputation to action in more personal terms. "When I heard about what Chuck Colson was doing with Prison Fellowship Ministries it sounded like something that Christians should be supporting, so I began to support it both personally and professionally."[60]

FRC's Perkins said his support for Nolan was based primarily on his own experiences serving as a prison guard when he was a young man. Despite FRC's religious emphasis, Perkins voiced skepticism about prison evangelism, having seen inmates manipulate spiritual opportunities. "Everybody had religion in the jailhouse," he said. His formative experience was more visceral: "I was locked in eight hours a day and saw the dehumanizing effect of the prisons," he said. "I saw the process from strip-searching, delousing, all that stuff that's dehumanizing, the body cavity searches, the whole thing . . . It was a shocking experience. There were a couple of situations, quasi-riots. The prison system I was in was under federal supervision because of previous problems. It was a shaping influence for me."[61]

Perkins believed his law-enforcement background reinforced Nolan's message. "People in the network know my background," he said. "It gives a little credibility to what Pat's doing. It's not just a weak, goody-goody thing—it's a legitimate approach to a growing problem." But the evangelical approach to prisons remains an important part of Perkins's vocabulary: "Where we come at this from an evangelical point of view," he said, "is these people have committed crimes, but they're still human beings, created in the image of God. Can we help them restore what's left of their lives?"[62]

In 2004, antitax activist Grover Norquist joined the cadre when he began attending a series of private, semi-regular meetings on criminal-justice reform with Nolan, Keene, and Viguerie, along with a small core of other conservative luminaries. As the president of Americans for Tax Reform and the ringleader of the Wednesday Group that brings together conservative activists on a weekly basis, Norquist has been one of the most important conservative coalition builders over the past two decades.[63] As noted in the preface, Norquist had thrown in his lot with the crime warriors in the early 1990s, penning an editorial that urged Republicans to seize on the issue as the political replacement for the Cold War.[64] But he had given signs over the years that his hostility to government could be turned on the justice system.[65] Like Keene, he had protested what he perceived as abuses of civil liberties by the Bush administration in the wake of the September 11, 2001, attacks, even collaborating with the ACLU. He had also privately expressed his support for Families Against Mandatory Minimums to Julie Stewart over the years, and she made a presentation at his Wednesday Meeting in the mid-2000s.[66]

As a result of listening to conservatives that he trusted, Norquist came around to the idea that the same principles he had about the rest of government should apply with equal force to criminal justice. "With national defense and with judicial—crime and prison—issues, a lot of conservatives, starting with me, assumed that the generals were sort of on top of how to handle this, and the prosecutors and the cops were on top of how to handle this," Norquist said. "They just needed resources, and they were doing reasonably good stuff with the money, and I focused on other things. Then, at some point, you look over and something jars you into, 'There's more to this.'" Norquist traces his concern over the issue in part to Chuck Colson, who made him aware of what prison life was really like. "There was this sense of prisons aren't reforming people. Prisons are unnecessarily abusive. You know, we didn't sentence you to 20 years to be beat up by other people. We sentenced you to go to jail for 20 years." He also cited a concern that many people were incarcerated for victimless crimes, such as drug or gun possession, and that the federal criminal law has expanded too much.[67]

Norquist's conversion did not come in a blinding, revelatory moment, but as a result of being hit from all sides over a long period of time. "You see this stuff coming like a mirage or something toward you. You see the issue, and then you see it again, and then you see it again. And then sometimes you just say, no, that's not a good idea ... And sometimes it just keeps moving into your sight," Norquist said, noting that the vision may look stronger when it is supplied by a friend. "When Dave Keene would say, 'What about this?' I'm willing to listen."[68]

What he is sure of, surprisingly, is that he was not converted to the cause because of its fiscal impact, but only deploys the argument because it resonates with state legislators. "The budget they run is teeny, and the prisons come out of their teeny budget. For me, who would like to see the whole cost of government down, fixing the entitlements just dwarfs this stuff. This is pennies. But if you're a legislator and the world you can control is limited, this is a huge lever," he said.[69] Norquist's story is not unusual among the core reform cadre of conservatives, none of whom cite fiscal concerns as a significant part of their reason for joining the cause.

The reform cadre began meeting regularly after Norquist and Keene separately approached Nolan at a 2004

Republican Party meeting and urged him to create a more structured forum for involving top conservative leaders in his work.[70] The discussions were held at the offices of the Carmen Group, a lobbying firm Keene worked for at the time. Regular participants at the working-group meetings included Brian Walsh, who worked with Meese at the Heritage Foundation; Eugene Meyer, president of the Federalist Society; and Tony Blankley, former press secretary to Newt Gingrich.[71]

The meetings were informal and designed to serve as brainstorming sessions; topics covered included overcriminalization, prisoner reentry, and pending federal legislation.[72] One gathering at the Heritage Foundation included then-GOP Senator Arlen Specter and focused on the idea of bringing any legislation that creates new criminal penalties under the jurisdiction of the Senate Judiciary Committee. The House of Representatives finally adopted a similar rule in January 2015.[73] Another proposal the participants batted around was to pare back the federal criminal law with a process modeled on the Base Realignment and Closure Commission, where Congress could take only and up-or-down vote on recommendations.[74]

The group's discussions were anchored by a strong sense that their role was to legitimate reform. "We found much greater consensus that we thought might have been there," Keene said. The question "was how we could make those views known to the broader movement, to make it in essence respectable, and . . . inhibit those who had a tendency to . . . jump on and exploit law and order."[75]

New, high-profile members entered the reform cadre in 2010. That year, former Congressman and Drug Enforcement Agency director Asa Hutchinson joined Keene, Norquist, and Nolan in endorsing a reform of crack-cocaine sentencing. Newt Gingrich also became involved. In January, Gingrich hosted a private discussion of sentencing issues at the American Enterprise Institute, with a guest list that included conservatives such as Nolan, Norquist, and the academic Lawrence Mead, as well liberals such as the academic Mark Kleiman and a deputy to Democratic Congresswoman Maxine Waters. Gingrich represents perhaps the clearest case of outright conversion among Nolan's associates. The man who once called for a World War II–like assault on the drug trade and championed prison construction in his Contract with America has become a strong critic of the justice system. "I think race has an enormous impact on decision after decision," Gingrich said in 2013, "and I think it would be very healthy for the country and for the Congress to re-evaluate . . . the whole way we've dealt with prison."[76]

Gingrich credits his development to Prison Fellowship's leaders and says he was strongly influenced by what he viewed as the efficacy of its Texas program in cutting recidivism. "You cannot describe the emergence of conservative thought about prison reform without the work of Chuck Colson and his faith-based ministry and then the work of Pat Nolan, and they were absolutely central, certainly, in my case. They educated me and brought me along and helped me much better understand things."[77]

By the beginning of the 2010s, the conservative reform cadre had become sufficiently large that law-and-order traditionalists no longer had a clear monopoly on the issue within the Republican Party.[78] The reformers had begun to clearly craft a distinct conservative frame for criminal justice that united evangelicals, libertarians, and fiscal conservatives around the idea that an inhumane, overreaching government threatened public safety and individual rights. Between the behind-the-scenes meet-ings of the early to mid-2000s and the public activism of 2010 and beyond, however, the politics of criminal justice in the states began to change. Eventually, this would pro-vide the opening that Nolan's cadre needed to crack the law-and-order consensus.

CHAPTER 5

Friends on the Outside

By the mid-2000s, conservatives such as Pat Nolan had developed the beginnings of a new language for criminal-justice reform and the core of an elite coalition to drive change at the national level. What they were still missing was a coherent, substantive package of reforms that were effective, comprehensive, and consistent with conservative ideology. They had an agenda, for sure, but not much of an alternative.[1]

This chapter traces how that alternative emerged. As it turns out, the package of ideas that conservatives have embraced in most states, known as the "Justice Reinvestment Initiative" (JRI), started out as a thoroughly liberal project to divert resources from criminal justice into social services for disadvantaged communities. The idea changed, however, as advocates began to sell JRI to real, working politicians. Out went diverting money from criminal justice and putting it into schools or health care. In came the notion that what JRI was really about was reallocating funds *within* criminal justice for greater cost effectiveness and better crime control. JRI was shorn of its "social justice" roots and rewired into a "performance" framework similar to that which conservatives and "New Democrats" have applied to other policy areas, such as education. At the same time, the JRI project moved from its original sponsor, the liberal Open Society Foundations, to a new set of organizations, with very different cultures: the Council of State Governments and the Pew Charitable Trusts.

CSG and Pew are technocratically oriented and almost obsessively bipartisan, and they advertise their work as "technical assistance." Both liberal and conservative politicians have, in fact, embraced JRI, and as we will see in chapter 8, the legislation the organizations work on tends to pass by overwhelming bipartisan majorities. Still, the JRI providers have done more than simply give conservatives a policy platform to rally around. The wonks at Pew and CSG quickly realized that their "technical assistance" would not drive criminal-justice reform on its own merits, and that the political unity their bosses craved would only survive if Republicans were carefully cultivated. So they worked behind the scenes to encourage the rise of the conservative reform movement, providing people like Nolan with ideas, visibility, and in Pew's case, funding. Conservative and technocratic agendas, therefore, have coevolved, a sharp contrast to the tough-on-crime era, when conservatives were skeptical of expert opinion or even hostile to it.

INVENTING JRI

In 1998, Eric Cadora was living in Brooklyn and feeling curious about how the neighborhoods around him had been affected by incarceration.[2] Cadora, who was working at a nonprofit that advocates alternative sentencing, began gathering data on the home addresses of inmates in New York's prisons. Over the years, he developed more and more detailed maps that ultimately led to a stunning result: in some neighborhoods, the government was spending over $1 million annually just to incarcerate the residents of a single block.[3]

In 2001, Cadora was invited to take his work to the Open Society Foundations, the left-leaning philanthropy run by the billionaire George Soros. OSF had been working on drug- and criminal-justice policy in a scattered way for several years, but was scaling up its commitment. At the time, this was a cause that few other foundations took an interest in. But OSF made the most of its Lone Ranger status, funding a range of initiatives that gave future leaders in criminal-justice reform a leg up, including Michelle Alexander, author of the 2010 bestseller *The New Jim Crow*; and Vanita Gupta, who led the ACLU's national project on mass incarceration before becoming an assistant attorney general.[4]

At OSF, Cadora's work on the neighborhood effects of incarceration began to meld with insights about what has been called the "correctional free lunch" generated by the fact that counties sentence felons and juveniles, but states pay to incarcerate them.[5] Cadora was deeply influenced by an innovative project in Oregon, where these incentives were inverted, so that the state paid a county for keeping wayward kids out of prison.[6] Cadora was also studying the Community Reinvestment Act, a landmark law requiring financial institutions to put some of their assets into low-income neighborhoods.

Thinking about the rewiring of incentives and the creation of local alternatives led Cadora to coin a new term, "justice reinvestment."[7] The basic idea was simple: to take money out of prisons and put it back into the neighborhoods that prisoners come from. Cadora and his boss, Susan Tucker, described the justice-reinvestment concept in a

2003 report. "The goal of justice reinvestment," they wrote, "is to redirect some portion of the $54 billion America now spends on prisons to rebuilding the human resources and physical infrastructure—the schools, healthcare facilities, parks, and public spaces—of neighborhoods devastated by high levels of incarceration."[8]

In this vision, justice reinvestment meant moving resources out of the criminal-justice system entirely, into "programs in education, health, job creation, and job training in low-income communities."[9] This was a classically left-liberal idea, in that it assumed that crime was essentially caused by social problems over which the tools of the criminal-justice system had little leverage, but human services did. The report also emphasized local control over the reappropriated funds, which it said would make communities responsible for their own public safety. Cadora said he hoped this would also create a demand for justice reform, rallying communities against mass incarceration by dangling a financial carrot in the form of state money for valued services.

But Cadora saw the rhetorical innovation of justice reinvestment as even more important than his substantive agenda. His primary goal, he says, was to develop a new language that would allow policymakers to escape the dichotomy of being hard or soft on crime. "It was so open rhetorically it just seemed like a good political title," he said. "What's not to like? Part of it [the political appeal] is that it doesn't mean anything."[10]

Cadora and Tucker's boss at OSF, Gara LaMarche, had his doubts. "As a practical matter," he said, "I thought the idea was a little utopian. [But] as a way of kind of helping people understand society's priorities, it was pretty compelling, and it had more legs than I thought at the time."[11]

THE ART OF THE POSSIBLE

Cadora and Tucker knew they needed someone with sharp political instincts to give shape to their ideas. They began consulting with Mike Thompson, the energetic director of justice programs for the Northeast region of the Council of State Governments, a nonprofit that promotes dialogue among state officials of all stripes.[12] Thompson was one of the future criminal-justice reform leaders who got an early boost from OSF. The foundation had funded him to launch a series of conversations with policymakers about "prisoner reentry," which positioned him to subsequently play an important role in Washington when Congress developed a major bill to address the topic.[13]

Thompson had joined CSG in 1997, and ever since, he had been hearing increasing frustration with tough-on-crime politics from state policymakers. By the early 2000s, Thompson said, legislators both left and right were asking him why prison costs kept climbing even as crime rates were falling. Justice reinvestment seemed like a potential answer, and Thompson got to work fleshing out the idea in a series of memos for OSF.[14] He argued that state and local officials urgently needed expert advice on managing their prison populations, a void that would have to be filled by support from foundations and the federal government:

> Sooner or later, officials in nearly every state will be unable to postpone a decision . . . about how to reduce their inmate population. And, these decisions will be made in the absence of research, consensus in the corrections (or, for that matter, law enforcement) community about how to best ensure offenders' successful transition to the community, and standards that establish how success will be measured. These decisions, then, will be

nearly blind ones—Russian Roulette with major public safety implications.[15]

In 2002, Thompson saw an opportunity to run the first big test of JRI in Connecticut.[16] The state had begun shipping prisoners to Virginia because of crowding, but the practice was highly controversial, especially after allegations surfaced that inmates had been mistreated. Meanwhile, the prison population continued to grow. The chairman of the House Judiciary Committee, Democrat Mike Lawlor of East Haven, was an active supporter of CSG's justice work, and now Thompson made him an offer: using funding from OSF and the JEHT Foundation, CSG would provide the state with criminal-justice guidance free of charge.

In 2003, CSG gave the Connecticut legislature a slate of recommendations that focused on moving parole-eligible inmates out of prisons sooner and finding ways to punish people who violated the terms of their probation with sanctions short of prison. The concept won support from Republican Gov. John Rowland, and many of the recommendations were adopted in a 2004 law.[17] Connecticut was able to end its contract with the Virginia prison and slash its inmate-housing budget by $27.9 million.[18]

But it also became clear that the "reinvestment" side of the equation was going to be tricky. Only $13.4 million of the savings went into reinvestment, and the bulk of that into various arms of criminal justice: $4 million for probation officers to supervise the larger number of offenders who were on the street instead of behind bars, a similar amount for halfway houses that would give released prisoners somewhere to go before they were cut loose, and close to $3 million to cut down the waiting list of inmates who needed a drug-treatment bed.[19] Just $1 million went into a pot for communities to spend on non-justice-related services, money that Thompson says immediately sunk into the muck of local politics, with little long-term impact.[20] Cadora recalls that "We didn't understand how to organize local communities." He even sought out ShoreBank, a Chicago-based "community development financial institution" as a potential partner to work out local strategy, but the efforts did not pan out.[21]

Still, CSG and OSF saw the Connecticut experience as a huge success. A state had passed legislation to reduce incarceration, and done so on the basis of careful analysis. "They didn't do a lot, but they did something that hadn't been done," Cadora said. Most importantly, legislators had developed a new language and a new narrative for thinking about incarceration.[22] "It was a sensational story," Thompson said. "Funders were thrilled."[23]

Meanwhile, Thompson was establishing a presence in Washington. With CSG's agenda expanding, the organization would need to pursue federal grants to finance its work. So Thompson hired a lobbyist, Barbara Comstock, who previously served as a spokeswoman for Bush's attorney general, John Ashcroft, and would go on to serve in Congress herself.[24] Here Thompson's work suddenly intersected with Pat Nolan's—though ironically, they were on different teams. Nolan was promoting legislation that aimed to reduce the incidence of rape in American prisons. Thompson and Comstock, meanwhile, negotiated on behalf of state corrections directors, who were skeptical of another unfunded mandate.[25] From that perch, CSG bargained for the creation of a grant program to help prison administrators offset the new PREA costs—and also for a pot of money that would fund future JRI reforms.[26] The "Protecting Inmates/Safeguarding Communities" program was established with a warrant that could reach well beyond the issue of rape: "to assist states and local jurisdictions in ensuring that budget cuts don't compromise efforts to protect inmates and to safeguard communities upon the inmate's reentry." The Bureau of Justice Assistance would later draw on the pot to kick-start Thompson's JRI work.

A NEW PATRON

While Thompson was shuttling between New Haven and Washington, a new player was contemplating whether to jump into the criminal-justice fray: the Pew Charitable Trusts. The foundation was a very different animal than OSF—much more concerned with bipartisanship and technocratic expertise, much less interested in grassroots advocacy and political controversy. One of the foundation's program officers, Lori Grange, was finding that legislators in deeply conservative states were growing impatient with the rising cost of incarceration, creating the potential for the strange-bedfellows alliances that Pew naturally gravitates toward. Among the people who caught her attention was Ray Allen, a Republican who chaired the corrections committee of the Texas House. As chapter 6 will discuss, Allen had pushed for downgrading basic drug-possession crimes from felonies to misdemeanors as early as 2003, amid a state budget crisis.[27] In fact, a number of states were taking administrative action to curb populations; Kansas, for example, made a sharp cut in its rate of parole revocations to prison.[28] Still, when Grange interviewed lawmakers like Allen, they told her over and over that they lacked the information to tackle the problem comprehensively. Grange argued that Pew could break open this policy area by providing expert, timely technical assistance while carefully cultivating conservative voices such as Allen's.[29]

As Grange's research progressed, Pew began holding meetings with organizations that were already doing similar work. One was the Vera Institute for Justice, a New York nonprofit that provides research and technical assistance on criminal justice. Pew was particularly interested in CSG's work in Connecticut because it provided a "proof of concept," a real case in which technical assistance helped produce a bipartisan breakthrough.[30] The group also seemed well positioned to make more magic happen. "Mike in particular seemed really savvy about . . . pulling together these different types of lawmakers," Grange said.

After a grueling three-year process, Grange finally won approval from the Pew board for a project that would develop an "evidence base" for state policymakers interested in reducing criminal-justice outlays, provide direct aid to those policymakers, and cultivate "unlikely bedfellows" coalitions.[31] To run the new project, Pew hired Adam Gelb, a vice president at the Georgia Council on Substance Abuse whose resume included stints running the Georgia Sentencing Commission, managing crime policy for the lieutenant governor of Maryland, and staffing the U.S. Senate Judiciary Committee.

Publicly, Pew debuted the project as based on three pillars, which still guide its work today: "Protecting public safety, holding offenders accountable, controlling corrections costs." The goal of reducing prison populations was framed as subsidiary to these pillars, and focused on low-level, nonviolent offenders. "A majority supports better, more cost-effective ways of holding low-level offenders accountable for their actions—and improving the likelihood they'll become productive members of society," Pew declared in its first brochure for the project.[32] It was, as Gelb observes, a deliberate choice to adopt a "return on investment versus a social, racial, economic, justice approach," one that kept the project in line with Pew's commitments, but also had a strategic purpose. The emphasis on offender accountability also marked a subtle reinterpretation of the justice reinvestment approach. While Cadora and Tucker had always acknowledged a role for parole and probation officers in their neighborhood-focused proposal, Gelb appeared to see much more clearly a need to shift resources from prisons directly into out-of-prison correctional supervision. "I don't think this is a 'eureka!' kind of notion," he reflected years later, "but I think a lot of the advocacy work in the field that preceded justice reinvestment paid woefully inadequate attention to the need to substitute incarceration with stronger supervision."[33]

Pew immediately began funding Vera and CSG to provide this technical assistance. OSF officials did not see this as an intrusion. "To make it a credible project this could not be simply a George Soros joint," Cadora said. "It wouldn't go very far." OSF was also in transition, restructuring its U.S. programs, and Cadora and Tucker were leaving the organization.[34]

With Pew's influence growing and OSF's waning, the initiative began drifting further away from the local reinvestment that had proven so difficult in Connecticut. As Thompson put it, "Pew was not at all sort of taken with the idea of reinvesting in particular neighborhoods or anything like that. And OSF would have never called their thing a 'Public Safety Performance Project.'" CSG did wire a strong local component into one of its next justice reinvestment projects, in Kansas, but again struggled to engage the target community.[35] As a result of these setbacks and shifting funder interests, justice reinvestment shed the most distinctively liberal parts of Cadora's original recipe— identifying the neighborhoods where most prisoners originate and reinvesting savings back in those places. At the same time, it acquired a stronger bias in favor of reinvesting the dollars saved by releasing inmates from prison into probation and parole. That was the price that had to be paid for following Pew's strategy, which focused on squeezing the most reform possible out of politicians' existing preferences, rather than organizing to try to fundamentally change them. This approach, which is further discussed in chapter 8, would later become a matter of significant aggravation among advocates on the left, but it was also essential to open doors for reformers on the right.

GOING CONSERVATIVE

In practice, Pew's goal of cultivating unlikely bedfellows translated into targeting conservatives, on the assumption that liberals were likely to already be on board. As Gelb put it, "Conservatives hold the cards on this issue, and we work closely with them."[36] Publicly, the foundation's primary mission would be analytic, helping politicians solve problems by providing nonpartisan expertise. But behind the scenes, Pew had to help create the demand for its own services by ensuring there was political space to consider alternatives, and conservatives would be key to that endeavor.[37] In fact, one of Pew's earliest grants, in August 2008, would go to Prison Fellowship and Pat Nolan.[38]

This reality was also apparent to the principals who had driven the Connecticut reforms. "Next was, we gotta go conservative," Cadora said. "We gotta go to a conservative state to do this." Still, it was as much serendipity as strategy that led CSG to its next two state projects, in Kansas and Texas. In Kansas, a moderate Republican legislator, Ward Loyd, had gotten in touch with Thompson after learning of the Connecticut story, and conversations showed that policymakers across state government were open to replicating the experiment. At the same time, CSG had developed a relationship with then-Senator Sam Brownback as a result of its involvement in congressional efforts to improve prisoner reentry. Thompson saw an opportunity to leverage that relationship in support of the cause. The Kansas JRI process kicked off with an event that featured speeches from both Democratic Gov. Kathleen Sebelius and the Republican Brownback, who would go on to succeed Sebelius as governor.[39]

Meanwhile, a freelance consultant who was working with CSG, Tony Fabelo, drew Thompson's attention to the possibility that Texas might also be willing to consider significant reforms. Thompson remembers thinking Texas was "the motherlode. God, if we can actually pull it off there—and talking to Tony I thought that maybe we could."[40] Not only would they pull it off, but they would kick off changes in other states that reformers once thought out of reach.

CHAPTER 6

Bull by the Horns

The Texas that George W. Bush left behind when he ascended to the presidency in 2001 was a poster child for rough justice. As governor, Bush had signed 152 execution warrants, a record even in a state where the death penalty was firmly entrenched.[1]

"Texas Tough" went beyond capital punishment. The Lone Star State had the nation's second-highest incarceration rate (after Louisiana), the second-largest inmate population (after California), and the second-fastest growth in prisoners during the 1990s (164 percent, behind only tiny Idaho).[2] All those "seconds" made for a clear superlative: when Americans thought about getting "tough" on crime, Texas was the example par excellence.

At its punitive height, however, Texas was about to get a rebranding, one that would provide an unassailably orthodox model for conservative reformers and spawn the most important criminal-justice reform organization on the right. Once Texas turned the corner in 2007, the politics of conservatives and mass incarceration would never be the same.

TOUGH ON CRIME, TEXAS STYLE

When the law-and-order panic swept the nation in the 1960s, the Democratic Party still dominated Texas politics, a legacy of the Jim Crow South's decades of one-party rule. But the state party's conservative establishment was being challenged by a liberal faction that quickly became allied with the Democrats' urban, northern wing, a partnership symbolized by the presidency of Lyndon Baines Johnson.

In response, some conservative leaders started to defect to the Republican Party, arguing that their former home had been taken over by a weak-kneed liberalism that encouraged crime and disorder. Others fought back from within the Democratic Party, criticizing their liberal co-partisans in terms that effectively confirmed the Republican attacks in voters' minds. Along the way, "law and order" emerged as the standard mantra of conservatives in *both* parties looking to rally electoral support.[3]

For example, U.S. Senator John Tower, the first Republican to win statewide office in Texas since Reconstruction, masterfully branded himself as a moderate conservative.[4] But that didn't stop him from embracing Goldwater's law-and-order agenda in a high-profile speech at the 1964 Republican National Convention, where he lamented, "We have come to the point where, in many cases, the lawbreakers are treated with loving-care."[5] When Tower won reelection in 1966 against conservative Democrat David Carr, the loser's response was to take up the law-and-order theme with newfound zeal.[6] And in 1970, conservative Lloyd Bentsen ousted liberal Senator Ralph Yarbrough in the Democratic primary by running an anti-liberal campaign emphasizing national issues including race and crime.

Texas crime politics took on a new dimension in 1981, when U.S. District Judge William Wayne Justice seized control of the state's entire prison system, determined to drag it from the era of plantation justice into something approaching modernity.[7] Among the judge's key reforms were strict limits on prison crowding.

The ban on playing sardines became the new linchpin of Texas crime politics as the state struggled to accommodate the rising tide of inmates washing in as a result of rising crime rates and aggressive prosecution tactics.[8] In the short term, the only way for state prisons to house incoming inmates without breaching the crowding was to let others out early, or to backlog people in county jails. Texas did plenty of both.

From 1978 to 1998, the two parties traded control of the governor's mansion back and forth in each election, with incumbents routinely finding themselves on the defensive about the crowding crisis. Initially, governors were reluctant to significantly hike prison spending, which left them vulnerable to attack. Democrat Mark White unseated incumbent Republican Bill Clements in 1982, in part by accusing him of mismanaging the prison litigation. Clements then turned the tables and retook the governorship in 1986, accusing White of releasing dangerous felons on parole to make room in the prisons.[9]

The years of crisis persuaded state leaders that the time had come to build more prisons. In 1987 Texas launched the first round of what would become a multiyear construction boom.[10] In 1990, Texas elected its first and only liberal governor—Democrat Ann Richards. Despite her progressive reputation, even Richards proved an eager jailor, attacking the Clements administration, which had added at least 26,500 beds to the prison system, for not building enough.[11] All the while, the crowding crisis was ongoing, and counties were suing the state for warehousing its inmates in their jails.[12]

Richards and legislative leaders mounted a massive response. At the governor's urging, Texas voters approved $1.1 billion for new cellblocks in 1991 and another $1 billion in 1993.[13] By 2000, those dollars had funded more than 82,000 new prison beds.[14] Richards did try to inject some reason into the process by calling for as many as 14,000 of those beds to be set aside for addiction treatment. But the treatment component was ultimately scaled back by more than half after an auditor found the state simply could not find enough qualified personnel to counsel more inmates.[15]

Meanwhile, the crime politicking went on. Even Richards's prison-building spree was not enough to hold off George W. Bush, who again played the "soft on crime" card to defeat the incumbent in 1994.[16] In office, Bush signed legislation making it easier to lock up low-level drug offenders and cracking down on juvenile delinquents.[17]

Rick Perry, who had served as Bush's lieutenant governor, took over where his predecessor left off. After assuming the governor's post in 2000, Perry was elected to a new term in a campaign that saw him accuse his Democratic opponent of planning to "cut the prison budget in half and release thousands of violent predators back on Texas streets."[18] Demagoguery, to be sure, but Perry was doing precisely what candidates of both parties were used to doing—furiously trying to get to the right of their opponents on criminal justice, and building up the state's prisons in the process. Intense political competition combined with the state's deep conservatism to produce an overheating machinery of punishment without an "off" switch.

THE NEW SHERIFFS

Just as Perry seemed to be confirming the punitive Texas consensus, however, that orthodoxy began to show its first, tentative cracks.

The first fissure was Tulia. On July 23, 1999, police in the tiny Panhandle town rounded up dozens of suspects, most of them black, and charged them with a range of drug offenses.[19] "Tulia's Streets Cleared of Garbage," the local paper declared the next day.[20] But as the world would eventually find out, the real story in Tulia was about law enforcement gone rogue. The charges were bogus, trumped up by local cops working under a grant from a federal program that critics say encourages drug arrests. The scandal broke open in 2000 and became a national story.[21] Texans were accustomed to outsiders huffing and puffing about the state's electric chair. But this was not a question of penal philosophy in which critics could easily be dismissed. For the first time, many legislators were forced to confront the reality of a law-enforcement machine that operated with perverse incentives and produced unjust results.

Tulia also marked a big opportunity for a liberal cadre of justice reformers that had convened in Austin in the late 1990s to push for police reform and had now embraced statewide ambitions. Scott Henson, a leader of the group, worked with liberal evangelicals to cleverly package the Tulia cause in ways that would appeal to religious conservatives, moving lawmakers to speak out on the floor about biblical prohibitions against bearing false witness. That year, the Texas legislature passed the so-called Tulia Corroboration Bill, which set new standards for testimony from undercover agents.[22] Lawmakers also approved a measure allowing the defendants to be freed on bond. (Rick Perry ultimately pardoned the last of them in 2003).[23] "There's a direct, linear connection between the left-right breakthrough on Tulia and everything that followed here," Henson later recalled. "Same people pushing it, mostly the same legislators pro and con, same strategies and tactics, same opposition howling like scalded hounds that they don't have automatic veto power anymore."[24]

The Tulia reckoning coincided with another remarkable turn in Texas criminal-justice policy: in the same 2001 session, the legislature rebuffed a proposal for new prisons. The Texas Department of Criminal Justice (TDCJ), which had grown fat and accustomed to expansion in the previous decade, had opened the two-year budget cycle by requesting nearly $100 million to build four new lockups. Fresh off the campaign trail, Perry endorsed the idea and stuck with it even after a state consultant said the prisons were unnecessary.[25]

The construction plan initially made sense to Pat Haggerty, an El Paso Republican who had led the House Corrections Committee since 1999. He started the job in "lock 'em up" mode, Haggerty said—but then began to examine the evidence. One fact that struck him was that thousands of offenders were mentally ill, in need of medical treatment more than incarceration. "That was one of the real reasons that I thought, 'Jesus, Mary and Joseph, this is all wrong,'" Haggerty says.[26]

Haggerty turned against Perry's proposal to build more prisons, and he managed to bring his legislative colleagues over to his side. Most people have no idea how prisons operate, and legislators are no exception, Haggerty said. "So when you finally sit down and explain it to them— they all got to the point where if . . . I was on the front mic and I was talking about prison issues, pretty much everybody went along and said, 'Okay, if you're for it then, hell, I can be for it, too.'"[27] It's a common situation in part-time legislatures whose members cannot possibly be up to speed on all the issues confronting them. Instead, they rely on shortcuts, either the word of a trusted colleague or a party orthodoxy that points to the "right" choice.

The legislature that reformed the Tulia drug laws and rejected the new prisons had still been under split party control, with Democrats ruling the House. But in 2003,

Republicans took over the lower chamber. It was the first time the GOP had ruled the House in a century, and it completed the party's sweep of state politics. Republicans controlled not only the legislature, but every major elected office in the state. Unified Democratic control had given way to unified Republican control, and there would be no reversal anytime soon.

Penal reformers did not despair, for they saw opportunity in the state's red turn. No longer did Republicans and Democrats have to compete over who was more conservative—the Republicans had decisively claimed that mantle. This gave the GOP room to experiment with unorthodox ideas. As Henson and his colleagues observed in a strategy paper the following year:

> In a "Nixon goes to China" scenario, Republican leadership has been able to take progressive positions on criminal justice reform that has [sic] sent Democrats—fearful of being labeled soft on crime—running for the door . . . Further, the Republican hegemony has created some pressure on candidates to distinguish themselves within the party. Criminal justice reform is providing that opportunity for many Republicans.[28]

The new majority was led by Tom Craddick, a driven businessman and hard-nosed negotiator from the oil town of Midland. Craddick had held his seat since 1969, and from that lonely perch he became one of the people most responsible for the statewide rise of the Texas GOP.[29] His first year as House Speaker was marked by epic partisan battles, including a redistricting fight that led a group of Democrats to flee the state in a bid to halt legislative business.

Perhaps the biggest headache confronting Craddick was a $10 billion budget shortfall, the product of a weak economy

combined with rising costs, especially for schools.[30] Every
state agency was ordered to trim its budget by double-digit
percentages, TDCJ included.[31] To make things worse, the
prisons were starting to fill up. Even after $2.3 billion in
construction, the state would soon run out of cell space.[32]

These problems were hoisted onto the shoulders of Ray
Allen, the man Craddick chose to run the House Criminal
Justice Committee. A staunch conservative, Allen proposed
privatizing a chunk of TDCJ operations to save cash.[33]
But Allen was also a veteran of the prison-spending battle
between Perry and the maverick Republicans two years
earlier. What is more, he had a strong relationship with
Scott Henson, which they developed while negotiating
issues of security and civil liberties in Texas in the wake
of the September 11, 2001, attacks. Now the duo began
talking criminal justice, and both say those conversations
significantly shaped Allen's thinking on the issue.[34] So
close was the relationship that Henson volunteered to work
for Allen's campaign when the representative later faced a
reelection challenge from an opponent who called him soft
on crime.[35] As a result of their talks, Allen supplemented
his privatization plan with several unorthodox measures,
including a proposal to downgrade basic drug-possession
crimes from felonies to misdemeanors.[36]

Perry, whose chief of staff was a former lobbyist for
Corrections Corporation of America, also wanted to pursue privatization. But Perry wanted to wring additional
budget reductions out of the agency's probation and parole
division. The governor, however, had not counted on Tony
Fabelo, the executive director of the Texas Criminal Justice
Policy Council. The Council was a state agency charged
with crunching the numbers on the prison system. Fabelo
had been running the Council for more than 20 years and
had earned a reputation for bipartisanship and straight talk

in Austin. Now, he warned that Perry's proposal would backfire. With less supervision, additional probationers and parolees would get into trouble and wind up behind bars, ultimately costing the state even more. If that wasn't enough to upset the governor, Fabelo also argued that privatization would generate marginal savings at best.

Perry dismissed the critique, but the legislature fought back, and the governor was forced to accept a compromise. The probation and parole cuts stayed in, but privatization was taken out. Meanwhile, drug possession would remain a felony, but first-time offenders would be given alternative sentences that would keep them out of prison.

At the end of the legislative session, the governor used his budget powers to shut down the Texas Criminal Justice Policy Council, an extreme case of a politician tuning out a message he doesn't want to hear. "They wanted me to cook the books," Fabelo said shortly after, "and when I said no, the bastards fired me."[37] But if Perry thought his purge would protect him from the reformers the next time around, he was wrong. In fact, Perry would soon find himself rushing to get to the front of their parade.

"DON'T BUILD MORE PRISONS"

In 2005, Craddick appointed a new chairman for the House Criminal Justice Committee, a cheerful Plano Republican named Jerry Madden. The speaker gave Madden simple instructions: "Don't build more prisons. They cost too much."[38]

Madden was a legislative veteran by Republican standards, but he had rarely thought about prisons. A native Iowan, he studied engineering at West Point, served in Vietnam, and took a job at Texas Instruments in Dallas in 1971. He spent most of the 1980s at a company that measured seismic activity, then moved his attention to the surface of the earth with a paving business he called Pothole Doc, before becoming an insurance salesman.[39] Madden represented Collin County, a wealthy northeastern Dallas suburb that was an early beachhead of Republican control in Texas.[40]

Nothing in Madden's record indicated that he was the kind of legislator likely to embrace criminal justice reform. Elected to the Texas House in 1992, he joined a group of GOP representatives who opposed forcing wealthy school districts to share revenues with poorer ones. Madden faced occasional primary challenges, but fended them off by high-lighting his conservative credentials. "I have an unmatched conservative and pro-business record," he boasted in 2001.[41] He later became chairman of the State Affairs Committee, which deals with controversial social issues. Madden used the perch to champion his pro-life position, press for a con-stitutional ban on gay marriage, and get the House to pass a bill calling for school textbooks to "reflect an overall tone that portrays the United States as a country that has over-come its mistakes and emerged as the freest, most demo-cratic nation in the history of the world."[42]

There was good news and bad news for Madden as he took up his new job. The state was not facing a budget crunch, but the prison system was once again filling up. By 2010, analysts warned, the prisons would be 10 percent overbooked.[43] It was a lot for a rookie to take in, so Madden quickly turned to an experienced veteran for help: his Senate counterpart John Whitmire, a Democrat who had been running that chamber's Criminal Justice Committee on and off since 1993.[44] (In Texas, members of the minor-ity party can chair legislative committees.) Whitmire had solid tough-on-crime credentials, having been one of the architects of the state's prison-construction program and a related overhaul of the penal code in the 1990s.[45] Whitmire had personal stakes in the issue: his family had been robbed at gunpoint in 1992. Under the old sentencing regime, Whitmire reflected in an op-ed three years later, their mugger was likely to do six years in prison—a stretch that, he wrote, "seems meager for the terror my family felt that night."[46] The senator added: "Sometimes, I think some of my colleagues and other elected officials need to be held up at gunpoint. Then they would take this as seriously as I do."[47]

Within a few years, however, Whitmire had realized that in the scramble to head off its crowding crisis the state overbuilt prison cells, and that it had failed to deliver on the treatment plans for nonviolent offenders he and Richards had envisioned.[48] By 2000, nonviolent offenders accounted for more than half the TDCJ population. For that group, Whitmire said, "we have got to get away from the notion that prison is the first solution."[49] Equally troubling to him was that two-thirds of prison admissions were the result of probation and parole violations, rather than new crimes.[50]

Madden and Whitmire swiftly agreed that fixing this pipeline from probation and parole into prisons should be their first priority. It was an obvious flaw, and an easier lift politically than reducing actual prison sentences. "If we go there," Madden said of sentencing, "we're jeopardizing everything else that we're doing."[51] Madden and Whitmire focused first on probation. Overloaded probation officers were unable to give high-risk offenders extra attention, so those people inevitably got into trouble, with nothing to do but ship them off to prison. Madden and Whitmire proposed cutting the maximum probation terms in half while hiring more officers, expanding drug courts, and setting up pilot programs that would use penalties short of prison to punish probation violations.[52]

The initiative at first got a warm reception, with even Rick Perry signaling interest. "There are better, more efficient ways to deal with this prison population than going and building more prisons," he said in February.[53] But opposition mounted as the details became clear. Prosecutors argued that it was not based on sound research and could backfire, because given the choice between shortened probation and prison, judges would often give an offender the latter. One district attorney dismissed estimates from legislative analysts that the measures could save the state $50 million as "a complete invention." Probation officials fretted that the plan would actually cost them money: offenders pay monthly fees for their supervision, and long-time probationers were considered some of the steadiest clients.[54] Madden and Whitmire scrambled to save the package, agreeing to scale back the types of crimes for which the shorter probation terms would apply.[55] The bill finally got through the legislature, but with significant opposition. In the House, the vote was 90-48, with two prosecutors-turned-legislators leading the bloc of dissenters.[56]

This proved too much for Perry. The governor vetoed the bill, citing the concerns of the state's district attorneys. "I can only conclude that their opposition stems from a good cause," he wrote in the veto proclamation, a reflection of the instinctive deference that Republicans still had for the views of prosecutors.[57] Perry did accept a $28.2 million increase in funding for probation officers and an additional $27 million for "residential treatment and sanction beds" that were included in the state budget, over which he had line-item veto power.[58]

Madden now says the veto was the best thing that could have happened to him, because it forced him to spend another two years tweaking his program. It was clear, however, that Perry had managed to rile the otherwise jolly representative from Plano. In an open letter to Perry, Madden accused the governor of failing to consult with him and Whitmire. Madden insisted his legislation had contained provisions that "are in fact very conservative," reflecting his confidence that reform could be sold on the right.[59] This belief would soon be the template for reform nationwide.

After he was axed by Perry, Fabelo went to work as a contractor for the Council of State Governments on its justice-reinvestment initiatives in other states. One day Fabelo, who was still living in Austin, bumped into Whitmire in the capitol, and the senator mentioned that he and Madden could use some help as they put together a second attempt at reform. Fabelo pitched the idea of working with Madden and Whitmire to CSG's Michael Thompson, who immediately saw the potential. And just like that, Fabelo was back in his element, crunching the numbers on Texas criminal justice.[60]

Fabelo ended up crafting the part of Madden and Whitmire's plan that would generate the most attention, a $240 million investment in alternatives to prison. That money created 8,000 slots for offenders with addictions to receive treatment, both behind bars and while free. Another 1,400 beds were added to so-called intermediate sanctions facilities, where people who violate the terms of their probation or parole can be locked up briefly instead of being sent back to prison to serve out complete sentences.[61] Meanwhile, Madden worked with advocates on the left and right to tweak the probation law that Perry had vetoed.

As the 2007 session started, TDCJ was back in trouble. The limited reforms of 2005 had cut prison admissions, but not enough to make a serious dent in the department's crowding problem. The prison system had been limping along on stopgap measures, but reality could not be put off much longer: Legislative analysts were forecasting a need for almost 18,000 new prison beds over the coming five years. TDCJ's response was to ask legislators for a bump in diversion funding—but also more than $378 million to build new cellblocks.[62] This time around, the money was actually available, with legislators expecting a $10 billion state surplus generated by economic growth.

When they learned what TDCJ had up its sleeve, Madden says, he and Whitmire requested a meeting with Perry. They saw him on the eve of his State of the State address, where he was set to introduce his new budget. In a meeting that lasted at least an hour, Madden says, they walked him through the details of their plan and persuaded him to give it a chance.[63] Perry bucked speculation that he would tout new prison construction in the speech, and instead included a line emphasizing diversion: "There are thousands of offenders in the system whose future we cannot ignore," Perry said. "Let's focus more resources on rehabilitating those offenders so we can ultimately spend less money locking them up again."[64]

This was Madden and Whitmire's year. The legislature approved ideas that would seem like long shots in Texas, such as a plan to fund nurse home visits and a measure allowing police to issue tickets rather than make arrests in some misdemeanor cases.[65] Even probation reform turned out to be much less contentious this time around. But there were still warts on the final product. Perry vetoed changes to the way probation is funded, which were designed to address the perverse incentives created when probationers pay fees for their own supervision. To get the diversion funding approved, Whitmire also had to cut a deal with Lieutenant Governor David Dewhurst, who was gearing up to run for U.S. Senate and supported the idea of new prison construction:

the budget would include funding *both* for the diversion plan *and* more than $230 million for three new prisons.[66] The deal created a fund TDCJ could tap if it decided that it needed more lockups after all. It never happened.

MAKING THE "TEXAS MODEL"

The bill that Texas passed in 2007 was hardly a reformer's dream, but it did represent an enormous shift in direction from Texas's past. Republican legislators and their governor had figured out how to use the word "rehabilitation" without choking, and they had established increasing levels of incarceration as a problem, rather than as the solution. They had turned the state ever so slowly away from its punitive past, and in doing so Republican politicians found that they were developing a taste for reform.

What is truly remarkable about Texas is that its incarceration rate, as shown in Figure 6.1, has declined considerably over the last decade while the national rate has only

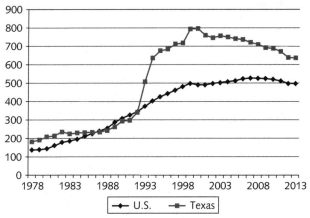

Figure 6-1 Texas versus National Incarceration Rates.
Source: Bureau of Justice Statistics, Corrections Statistical Analysis Tool, http://www.bjs.gov/index.cfm?ty=nps.

flattened out. Of course, Texas was starting from a much higher baseline. The downward trend began before 2007, driven in part by a slightly more generous parole policy. But 2007 is widely seen as the turning point. Since then, Texas politicians have closed three prisons—and boasted about it rather than running for cover. "You want to talk about real conservative governance?," Perry said in 2014. "Shut prisons down. Save that money."[67] Meanwhile, Texas legislators have passed laws allowing offenders to earn time off their sentences, limiting employers' liability for hiring ex-offenders, and increasing the monetary thresholds for property crimes.[68] In 2014, the Texas Association of Business helped launch a "Smart on Crime Coalition" that advocates for more such policies.[69]

Important as the 2007 law was inside Texas, its more impressive impact was on the rest of the country. The technocrats at Pew and CSG, who were beginning their ambitious program to underwrite sentencing reforms across the country, immediately recognized that the Texas program had the makings of a PR coup. As Pew's Adam Gelb put it, "People think if Texas does something, by definition it's not going to be soft."[70]

The reformers began by telling their success story on Capitol Hill. CSG had developed ties to several lawmakers in Washington through its work on the Prison Rape Elimination Act and prisoner reentry, and now directed its attention to the "man-bites-dog" stories of Texas and Kansas, where it had also shepherded through a reform package. The chair and ranking member of the House subcommittee charged with justice funding, Al Mollohan of West Virginia and Republican Frank Wolf of Virginia, held a hearing on Texas and Kansas in April 2009 and later that year appropriated $10 million to fund similar CSG initiatives in other states. Mollohan and Wolf were not the only representatives the JRI reformers impressed. California Democrat Adam Schiff and his Republican colleague Dan Lungren (who had engineered the passage of major tough-on-crime legislation in the 1980s) proposed a bill of their own in November 2009 to fund JRI to the tune of $35 million annually.[71]

Meanwhile, Jerry Madden's reform work did not go unpunished. In 2008, he faced a primary challenge from a 23-year-old who accused him of being soft on crime. Madden won the race, but it was his tightest primary contest ever.[72] On the national stage, however, he was being honored as the new face of conservative reform. Madden became a frequent speaker at meetings of American Legislative Exchange Council (ALEC) and National Conference of State Legislatures (NCSL); *Governing* magazine named him and Whitmire "Public Officials of the Year" in 2010. In 2011, facing two challengers in his next primary, Madden announced his retirement.[73] Although he was leaving the Texas legislature, his involvement in criminal-justice reform was just beginning.

CHAPTER 7

A Vast Right-Wing Conspiracy

Jerry Madden likes to remind audiences that his background was in engineering, not criminal justice, which made his assignment to lead the House Corrections Committee less than thrilling. His first thought, Madden recalls, was a despairing, "Why me?" But Madden says he began applying engineering principles to the mission that Speaker Tom Craddick had given him: "Don't build more prisons." It quickly became obvious there were only two ways to keep the state's inmate population in check: "Slow 'em down coming in, or speed 'em up coming out."[1] The latter option was a non-starter, Madden continues, so Texas devoted itself to the first.

To hear this tale from the jovial Madden, now in his early '70s, is a bit like having your favorite uncle walk you through a home-improvement project. Madden's knack for storytelling, combined with his conservative credentials, made him one of the most important spokespersons for criminal-justice reform in recent years, traveling the nation to tell the story of the Texas turnaround. His barnstorming is part of a much larger campaign, in which conservative

Texans have teamed up with Pat Nolan's Washington network and the technocrats at Pew to rebrand prison reform as a right-wing cause.

Together, these three partners rewired conservative ideas and institutions on criminal justice in ways that were previously unimaginable. They penetrated conservative policy shops, most notably the American Legislative Exchange Council, notorious among liberals for its aggressive opposition to gun control and its history of schmoozing with private-prison operators. And they launched a national publicity campaign that put the reputations of Nolan and his allies behind the cause like never before.

Each partner in this triumvirate contributed something unique. The Texans had a good yarn to tell about curbing prison growth in a place famous for its rough justice, and they had connections to conservatives in other states. Nolan had the identity-vouching power of his friends and access in the corridors of power in Washington. Pew had the wonkish expertise and management skills to coordinate a multipronged reform campaign, along with money that conservative donors were not yet ready to commit.

Their combined effort has scaled up the identity vouching that Chuck Colson first practiced among religious conservatives and Nolan deployed ad hoc to move the needle in Washington. The cause of rolling back incarceration is now being promoted to the national movement as the new orthodoxy, tested in the conservative proving ground of Texas and guaranteed by conservative legends, such as Grover Norquist, as well as new stars, such as Tea Party leader Erick Erickson.[2]

The process of identity vouching that came together in the form of Right on Crime demonstrates just how important resources, reputations, and strategic acumen are to the process of changing party positions. Most of the resources that supported this initiative came, at least initially, from outside the conservative movement— it could never have had the impact it did without the money that centrist and left-leaning foundations were willing to put into it. The heart of the campaign, however, was the conservative identity of its spokespeople. Not just anyone could have done this work, since it leveraged individual and organizational reputations within the conservative movement that were produced over decades. Finally, all of this would have been for naught if it were not for a number of critical strategic choices, the most important of which was to protect the ideological reputation of the movement's leaders, by keeping their relationships to reformers on the left behind the scenes.

A LONE RANGER MAKES FRIENDS

The organizational core of the new wave of reform activity was the Austin-based Texas Public Policy Foundation. TPPF is the largest member of the State Policy Network, an alliance of state-level think tanks with generally libertarian leanings, and has always had a reputation as one of its most ideologically uncompromising affiliates. For example, TPPF came to public attention as the source of Gov. Rick Perry's proposals for more "business-like" management of Texas universities and efforts to roll back regulation in the Lone Star State and cut its already-lean budget.[3] If TPPF was behind something, conservatives could be sure it was ideologically solid. The think tank's influence is manifest in the ties it maintains to other SPN groups. In a survey of 27 SPN member organizations conducted for this book, nearly a quarter listed TPPF as one of the three organizations they work with most closely, making it the most popular among the state think tanks.[4]

In 2005, as Madden and Whitmire began their legislative partnership, TPPF launched a "Center for Effective Justice" to promote a conservative vision of criminal-justice reform. The center was the brainchild of Tim Dunn, a TPPF board member. Dunn is a major political donor, known for bankrolling the antitax watchdog Empower Texas and financing primary challenges aimed at insufficiently conservative Republican legislators.[5] Dunn's conservatism, which combines evangelical faith with an austere vision of government, has led him to a scathing critique of the criminal-justice system as statist rather than victim oriented. He illustrates the argument by positing the case of a theft victim, who simply wants her property returned and an acknowledgment of remorse from the perpetrator. Instead, the state is just as likely to impound the property while locking the offender out of sight, at taxpayer expense. As a result, Dunn says, "the victim gets mugged twice." His conclusion: "Our criminal justice system is more suitable to a tyranny. We don't focus on restoring the victim; we are focused on crushing the life of the perpetrator."[6] Dunn said his views on criminal justice were deeply influenced by the work of Charles Colson. When he called Prison Fellowship in the mid-2000s asking for a package of statutory recommendations, however, they had none to offer. That is what prompted the idea of the Center for Effective Justice.[7]

To turn its limited-government philosophy into a concrete program for justice reform, TPPF hired Marc Levin, a libertarian just three years out of the University of Texas law school. Levin had no background in criminal justice, but he proved to be a quick study. By 2007, he was one of the handful of wonks that Texas lawmakers routinely turned to for advice, even earning a commendation from the legislature for his contributions to that year's reform.[8] But Levin's most important work came after the session, when he began spreading the word about what Texas had accomplished.

Most SPN think tanks only have the bandwidth to specialize in one or two major issues. On other matters, they tend to borrow the positions and research of sister organizations with a specialty in the area.[9] Once TPPF planted its flag on criminal justice reform, therefore, its position could quickly become authoritative for all the other organizations in the network. As the only SPN think tank that had a full-time staffer working on criminal justice, TPPF soon became the movement's nerve center on the issue.

Levin initially shared his insights with colleagues at other SPN think tanks informally, as the opportunity arose. But he soon began talking with Fabelo and Thompson, the Council of State Governments officials whose ideas were at the core of the Texas reforms, about making a systematic push. They looped in Pew, and by 2008, the foundation had awarded Levin a grant to spread the Texas story, in part through SPN.[10] At an SPN conference in Washington that December, Levin hosted a seminar on criminal-justice reform attended by almost 50 people representing 36 think tanks.[11] Over the following year, the same grant took him to Colorado, Ohio, and South Carolina to help local SPN think tanks host similar events for their legislators and pundits.[12]

Levin was not the only Texan building a national profile based on the state's success story, however. When Jerry Madden hit the reform jackpot, CSG and Pew also began sending him to various forums to share his story. Between 2007 and 2009, Madden spoke at a congressional hearing and at events in Florida, Washington state, and both Carolinas. He was named vice chairman, and later chairman, of the criminal-justice committee of the bipartisan National Conference of State Legislators.[13] And while

Levin courted his colleagues at the State Policy Network, Madden began to lead a change at an even unlikelier target: the American Legislative Exchange Council (ALEC).

SMART-ALEC?

The American Legislative Exchange Council became notorious in 2012 when the killing of the unarmed black teenager Trayvon Martin by a Florida neighborhood-watch member drew attention to the group's aggressive pro-gun stance. A conservative association of state legislators and businesses, ALEC has enjoyed great success since the 1990s in creating "model legislation" for lawmakers in state after state. For Republican state legislators who know they are conservative but do not know what positions to take on a range of unfamiliar issues, ALEC's model legislation provides an immediate signal of orthodoxy and a template for action. These tools are especially important given the limited time, experience, and staff of most state lawmakers.[14]

ALEC focuses primarily on economic issues, but to critics on the left the organization is better known for promoting the "stand-your-ground" legislation that became infamous after the Martin shooting in Florida, and for hawking harsh penal policies while taking sponsorship dollars from private-prison operators. There is, in fact, a strong connection between these two positions. Throughout the 1990s, ALEC delegated them to the same internal "Public Safety and Elections Task Force," which included representatives of the National Rifle Association (NRA). The NRA was advocating an aggressive penal program it dubbed "CrimeStrike," designed to fend off arguments that loose gun laws were responsible for the nation's crime problem.[15] The real cause of violence, NRA leaders argued, was not a surfeit of guns, but a shortage of prisons.[16] The task force also included representatives of the Corrections Corporation of America, which obviously stood to gain from model bills that would increase incarceration and promote the use of private prisons.[17] In 1994, ALEC released a widely publicized study that concluded, "getting tough works."[18] Promoting the report, former Reagan Attorney General William Barr declared, "Increasing prison capacity is the single most effective strategy for controlling crime."[19] Throughout the decade, ALEC would create model bills advocating more incarceration through devices such as "three strikes" and "truth-in-sentencing."[20]

This iron-fisted past hardly positioned ALEC as a natural candidate to support reductions of prison populations. But that is precisely what has happened. The first public sign of a new wind blowing through ALEC's corridors came from Ray Allen, the Texas legislator who preceded Jerry Madden as chair of the House Corrections Committee. Allen also served on ALEC's public-safety task force, and in a 2004 ALEC publication, he declared, "Corrections policy in the coming decades cannot sustain the long-term financial costs associated with over-reliance on prisons as a means of controlling crime ... Doctors don't perform surgery or hospitalize patients if less invasive, less costly therapies will restore their patients to health, and likewise, prison beds, because of their high cost to build, maintain and operate, ought to be treated as an option of last resort within a more expansive range of options."[21]

That perspective would grow in power, thanks to the influence of Pat Nolan and Jerry Madden. Nolan was a longtime friend of ALEC, which named him a "Legislator of the Year" before his incarceration. After he began working for Prison Fellowship, Nolan was invited to join the public-safety task force, where one of his early victories was persuading the organization to endorse the

Second Chance Act, federal legislation to help released inmates transition out of prison (which will be discussed in chapter 9). While largely symbolic, the move represented a significant shift in the framing ALEC brought to issues of crime and punishment. Whereas ALEC's 1994 report had declared that "scarce public funds" should be focused on "increasing incarceration rates, particularly for violent offenders," the group now argued that reducing corrections costs would require the "safe and successful re-integration of individuals who have been incarcerated."[22]

In 2007, ALEC hired Michael Hough, a former Maryland legislative aide and Nolan confidant, to staff the public-safety task force. Nolan takes no credit for the hire, but Hough brought a reformist outlook to the position, and their close relationship surely didn't hurt the cause. Meanwhile, Madden began telling the story of the 2007 Texas reforms at ALEC meetings. After a 2009 presentation in Atlanta, the three men huddled at a restaurant to consider next steps. They decided to launch a model-legislation project focused on criminal-justice reform.[23] That September, they started a new subcommittee of the public-safety task force focused on "Corrections and Reentry." A wave of reform-minded proposals followed, including allowing non-prison sanctions for probation violations, letting offenders earn time off probation, encouraging employers to hire ex-offenders, restricting asset forfeiture, and allowing departures from mandatory minimums for nonviolent crimes.[24] The new direction was spurred along by Pew. The foundation donated more than $200,000 to ALEC between 2010 and 2011, and its proposals served as a template for some of ALEC's model bills. Meanwhile, ALEC dropped all of its earlier model legislation that called for harsh punishment—more or less starting from scratch.[25]

In 2012, the Martin killing almost put an end to ALEC's criminal-justice work. In the aftermath of the teen's death, ALEC came under intense attack for the role it played in the passage of Florida's "Stand Your Ground" law in 2005. ALEC responded by initially cutting the Public Safety and Elections Task Force entirely, in order to focus more narrowly on economic issues. Just a few months later, however, ALEC resuscitated its justice reform effort as the "Justice Performance Project." Tellingly, the moniker is almost identical to the name Pew gives its JRI work: "Public Safety Performance Project."

Michael Hough, who by 2012 was a Maryland state legislator, said that Nolan, Madden, and he were able to convince ALEC to keep the organization engaged on criminal justice by arguing that the issue is central to the state budget matters that are ALEC's bread and butter. "Hey, it is a fiscal issue. It's not a social issue. It's a fiscal issue, just like Medicare or education. It's in the state budget, so it's important."[26] Just as important was the impact that restarting this work might have on ALEC's damaged organizational reputation. "It was an area where we were able to work across party lines and work with non-traditional allies," Hough said, recalling an early meeting with the ACLU. "Some of the groups there might have been the ones that said ... ALEC is this boogeyman. When we got down and actually started talking about the issues ... even our harshest critics acknowledge that ... they agree with us here on this issue."[27]

The composition of the Justice Performance Project looks different from that of the old public-safety committee. The private-prison companies that loomed so large to critics in the past had left ALEC by March 2012.[28] That same year, meanwhile, Families Against Mandatory Minimums joined the organization to support its reform push.[29] That does not mean ALEC has stopped working with interests that have a financial stake in criminal-justice policy. The organization maintains a tight embrace with commercial bail bondsmen (who charge pre-trial defendants hefty fees to post the collateral that gets them out of jail). As of September 2015, about one-fifth of ALEC's 37 model bills on criminal justice were provisions favorable to the bail industry.[30] They included legislation creating "post-conviction bonds" that would be used for a type of parole, a potentially massive market expansion that has since been proposed in at least 14 states and passed into law in Mississippi.[31] ALEC has also passed crime-related measures suggested by task-force members representing other interests, such as the maker of an anti-addiction drug, a DNA-testing service, and the stun-gun manufacturer Taser International Inc.[32]

There is ample room, in other words, to dismiss ALEC's reform drive as mere opportunism, a shift from one set of corporate patrons to another. But the sequence of events, the biographies of the people involved, and the content of what has been passed suggests that ideological change was primary in this story, and that the change will be durable. ALEC certainly has not converged on the liberal criminal justice position. Its advocacy on behalf of the bail industry may well have the effect of "widening the net" of criminal sanctions even if they become less severe, and could complicate efforts to fix local jails. Nonetheless, ALEC has contributed significantly to helping brand criminal justice reform as "conservative," giving reformers powerful access in state capitals.

THE BIG ROLLOUT

Marc Levin's shop was turning into a success story. SPN think tanks from West Virginia to Montana were calling him for advice and spotlighting justice reform in their own publications and meetings with legislators.[33] Levin was starting to become popular with editors, too. In 2008 alone, the Center for Effective Justice was featured in 45 media outlets, according to TPPF's count.[34]

It was clear, in other words, that the man-bites-dog story Levin had to tell could get even bigger. In December 2009, Levin and Pew's Adam Gelb were both at a conference in San Diego and held a poolside meeting at their hotel to talk about next steps. They settled upon an idea that effectively fused the reform cadre Pat Nolan had developed in Washington with the state-level network being cultivated by the Texans. The plan was to draft a "Statement of Principles" on criminal justice that would be publicly endorsed by Nolan's associates and publicized in an ongoing campaign by TPPF. The effort would be dubbed "Right on Crime" and would include a comprehensive website featuring testimonials, news, policy briefs, video of events, and the like. As Gelb explains, "A handful of conservatives across the country were starting to talk about criminal justice reform. The idea behind Right on Crime was to organize, amplify and multiply them."[35]

Looping in Nolan was a simple matter. Pew had been funding Nolan's work since August 2008, and he had gotten to know Levin over dinner during a previous trip to Austin. "I laugh and say we're like twins separated at birth," Nolan said. "We agreed on everything. You couldn't put a piece of paper between us."[36] Right on Crime was unveiled in December 2010. The following month, Gingrich and Nolan declared in a *Washington Post* op-ed, "The criminal justice system is broken, and conservatives must lead the way in fixing it."[37]

While Nolan had previously rallied his associates to publicly support individual causes, this was the moment at which they declared a fundamental change in the conservative approach to crime. As the Statement of Principles put it, "Conservatives correctly insist that government services be evaluated on whether they produce the best possible results at the lowest possible cost, but too often this lens of accountability has not focused as much on public safety policies as other areas of government." The statement condemns the criminal-justice system as a government program "that grows when it fails." Instead, it argues, "An ideal criminal justice system works to reform amenable offenders who will return to society through harnessing the power of families, charities, faith-based groups, and communities."[38] As of October 2013, the Right on Crime "Statement of Principles" had over 60 signatories; Figure 7-1 lists some of the most prominent.[39]

The Right on Crime statement is a textbook case of identity vouching, designed both to motivate conservative policymakers by making justice reform an ideologically safe issue and to reassure them that it is electorally safe. As Levin wrote in a grant application describing the project, Right on Crime "provides a durable, high-profile platform through which we can leverage the credibility of the prominent conservative leaders and organizations that are involved to provide not only the intellectual ammunition, but also the political cover that policymakers often need to make the right choices in criminal justice policy."[40]

Also in 2010, Keene and Nolan took a less public, but perhaps even more significant, step to vouch for the reform movement, working with Virginia Sloan's bipartisan non-profit, the Constitution Project. In the run-up to the 2010 elections, the Constitution Project collaborated with the Republican Governors Association and the Democratic Governors Association to urge all major-party gubernatorial candidates to embrace the reform movement. The letter

Gary Bauer	President, American Values
William Bennett	Former education secretary and "drug czar"
Jeb Bush	Former Florida governor
Chuck Colson	Founder, Prison Fellowship
Ken Cuccinelli	Former Virginia attorney general and GOP gubernatorial candidate
John J. DiIulio	Former director of White House Office of Faith-Based and Community Initiatives
Robert Ehrlich	Former Maryland governor
Erick Erickson	RedState.com editor-in-chief
Newt Gingrich	Former Speaker of U.S. House
Asa Hutchinson	Former Drug Enforcement Agency administrator and Arkansas congressman
David Keene	Former American Conservative Union chairman and NRA president; editor at *Washington Times*
Edwin Meese III	Former attorney general
Stephen Moore	Founder of Club for Growth
Pat Nolan	American Conservative Union (formerly Prison Fellowship)
Grover Norquist	Americans for Tax Reform president
Tony Perkins	Family Research Council president
Ralph Reed	Faith and Freedom Coalition founder; former Christian Coalition executive director
Richard Viguerie	Chairman, ConservativeHQ.com
J. C. Watts	Former congressman from Oklahoma

Figure 7-1 Prominent Right on Crime "Statement of Principles" signatories.

to Republican candidates was signed by RGA Executive Director Nick Ayres and cited Nolan, Keene, and former New Jersey Attorney General Anne Milgram as supporters of the initiative. "*Do not box yourself in* during the campaign by promising to build more prisons or to support laws that increase sentences for non-violent offenders," an accompanying information sheet from the Constitution Project urged.[41] The RGA letter said that five governors-elect would receive free technical assistance on "policy development and strategic communications that will place candidates seeking to cut corrections spending, lower crime and secure public safety, in the best possible position to accomplish those goals as Governor." That aid, the letter added, would be funded by the Public Welfare Foundation—a liberal donor that has also supported Right on Crime.[42] The RGA at the time was chaired by Mississippi Governor Haley Barbour, a longtime associate of Keene's, who had quietly cut back incarceration significantly in Mississippi.[43] Similar messages went to Democrats with the endorsement of Mark White, a conservative Democrat and former Texas governor who has long been an advisor to the Constitution Project.

A NEW CONVENTIONAL WISDOM

Fifty years after Barry Goldwater touched off the "law and order" era in American politics, the United States has a new conservative orthodoxy on criminal justice. SPN, ALEC, Right on Crime, and Prison Fellowship have helped diffuse a distinct conservative language for criminal-justice reform, one that allows movement supporters to endorse measures such as reductions in sentences and reentry programs without being viewed as moving to the center ideologically. This is vital in an era when moderation or bipartisanship is political poison.

The new conservative critique of criminal justice asserts that prisons and police are just as much a part of government as any other agency, and hence their growth should be viewed with the same skepticism as any other expansion of state power. In Pennsylvania, for example, conservative activist Matthew Brouillette coauthored an op-ed arguing that "unprecedented [prison] population growth was caused not by an increase in crime, but by a bureaucratic breakdown."[44] In this new, more aggressively libertarian formulation, everything government touches is under suspicion. Conservatives have argued for decades that government functions like education should be judged by "outputs" rather than "inputs," and that generating results requires applying strict accountability measures to generally untrustworthy public servants, lest they simply expand their empires without adding public value. The innovation of Right on Crime and its allies is extending this critique, which has typically been aimed at the welfare state, to the criminal-justice system.

Through their writing in conservative publications, newsletters targeted at legislators, speeches at major events like the Conservative Political Action Conference, and events in state capitols, conservative reformers have made easily available to politicians the lifeblood of politics—clichés. Their new frame for criminal justice has become a standard discourse, part of the package of conservative talking points that politicians adopt without deep consideration. Conservatives in many different places use the same phrases again and again in describing their efforts: The right's leadership on criminal justice reform is "like Nixon going to China."[45] Police officers and prison wardens are just "bureaucrats with guns."[46] Prisons are like Kevin Costner's *Field of Dreams*: "If you build it, [they] will come."[47] In Georgia, a news article critically noted that several politicians had used another line we have heard frequently in interviews: "We should be locking up the people we're afraid of, not the people we're mad at." The story alleged that the politicians had swiped this slogan from an ALEC presentation, but it has become so familiar that it is impossible to trace where an individual reformer first heard it.[48] The repetitive quality of these phrases is a strong indication of an increasingly self-conscious and coordinated movement (in much the same way that the coordination of education reformers can be seen in the regular way in which they use phrases such as "education is the civil rights issue of our time," or "schools should be about the kids and not the grown-ups").[49] When combined with the moralistic framing of evangelicals, the public choice critique provides a powerful, indigenous foundation for rethinking mass incarceration.

Crucially, this rhetorical strategy is one of ideological purification—conservatives were inconsistent before, so that by becoming more critical of incarceration they are correcting deviations from orthodoxy in the past. In fact, reformers have been at pains not to openly abandon the older "tough-on-crime" rhetoric that proved so central to conservative identity, and would thus be dangerous to confront directly. Family Research Council's Tony Perkins, for example, said, "It's not just a weak, goody-goody thing . . . I'm not weak on crime. We have to take a hard line. We've got some really serious crime issues in this country, so I'm not weak."[50] In a speech to ALEC members, Norquist said, "There's no bleeding heart whatsoever . . . This is not moving to the center. This is not being reasonable. This is not being moderate, or any of this nonsense."[51] In an interview, Norquist lambasted Democrats as lacking any credibility on the issue, a continuation of his rhetoric from the 1990s. To the extent the reformers acknowledge they have changed their position, then, it is only to stress that they have become more faithful to conservative identity, and indeed more committed to their original cause of fighting crime.[52]

All of these clichés have permitted conservative politicians to easily explain to themselves, and their supporters, why they are doing things that just a few years ago would have seemed unforgivably liberal. While experts in the field might be tired of hearing these talking points repeated ad nauseum, they provide what working politicians crave, which is familiarity. The notion that the United States unnecessarily incarcerates far too many people is becoming standard conservative fare, rather than a pathbreaking proposition.

CHAPTER 8

Red-State Rehabilitation

Nathan Deal was tearing up.

It was May 2012, and the Georgia governor was signing legislation hailed as one of the most sweeping criminal-justice reforms in the nation. Deal's eyes went moist as he recalled attending "graduation" ceremonies at a drug court run by his son, Jason.

"To listen to the stories, to the lives that have been changed, the families who have been reunited and lives that have, quite frankly, been cast aside by the system that was in place, had a tremendous emotional effect on me," Deal said.[1]

The intensity of Deal's commitment to the cause was extraordinary, and as a result, Georgia has taken criminal justice reform further than most states. The reform drives in Georgia—and Texas before it—are not mere flukes, however; they are the strongest indicators of a trend sweeping across conservative America. As Republicans consolidate their control of right-leaning states, the temptation to pound the crime issue fades. Each time a new conservative state joins the club of justice reformers, and finds itself celebrated by the Right on Crime campaign, pressure grows on others to follow suit. And when a state does dip a toe in the water and break down the barriers to recognizing the problems with mass incarceration, it becomes easier to promote further reform in subsequent rounds.

With the old get-tough frames all but evaporated, conservatism has taken on a more analytical mode of policymaking. The potential and limits of that new policymaking style are on full display in Nathan Deal's Georgia.

FINDING RELIGION ON JUSTICE REFORM

Before Pew agrees to work with a state, the organization tries to ensure that it has a "champion," a well-placed politician who is highly committed to justice reform. These champions come to the cause by different routes. Some, like Jerry Madden, are intrigued by the analytical problem, while others, like Deal, are driven by much more personal motivations. However they come to the cause, conservative champions are increasingly finding the road they travel to be well paved and friendly, thanks to the investments Pew has made in the conservative infrastructure of ideas.

When Nathan Deal ran for Georgia governor in 2010, he touted his hostility to illegal immigration and his business-friendly bona fides but was silent on corrections.[2] Behind the scenes, however, the candidate was boning up on the crisis in the Georgia justice system. In his prior careers as a prosecutor and juvenile-court judge, Deal had seen enough of the system to know that something was wrong. "Many times, the repeat pattern of offenders was generational," Deal said. "You would see juveniles, and then later you would see them as adults, coming back through our system."

Deal was also heavily influenced by visits to his son's drug court, which convinced him that people who were given a second chance could be rehabilitated.[3] This was in direct contrast to the earlier conservative conventional wisdom that, other than prisons, "nothing works" and that rehabilitation was a liberal delusion.[4]

Finally, Deal had been shocked by a widely publicized 2009 Pew report that found 1 in 13 Georgians were under some form of correctional supervision, more than twice the national average and nearly three times the rate of 1982.[5] As the candidate dug deeper, "he found some numbers about what's going on here in Georgia that he just believed to be absolutely staggering," said Thomas Worthy, a former Deal aide who became his point man on criminal justice.[6]

Deal was joined in the conservative criminal justice reform cause by Jay Neal, a pastor-turned-legislator from the small North Georgia town of Lafayette. Until about 15 years ago, Neal embraced the conventional wisdom about addicts. "I didn't have very much use for them, to be honest with you," Neal says. "I kind of had that feeling that if they can't do this on their own, then we need to help them, and ... that means locking them up and teach them a lesson. If they don't get it, then we must not have locked them up long enough."[7]

In 2001, Neal decided to run for the state legislature. Around the same time, the director of an addiction-recovery house in his district asked Neal to join the board of the organization. Neal agreed, figuring the position was a way to buff his community-service resume as he campaigned for office. But then something happened that Neal had not counted on: men from the recovery house began attending Neal's church. And after they had been worshipping with his congregation for a while, they asked to join—25 of them at once. Neal now faced the prospect of enlarging his tiny congregation by 50 percent, with all the new members being drug addicts.

"I kind of saw that as God inviting us to be involved in his work, so I was okay with it," Neal recalled. "But at the same time, I didn't want to do it unless my congregation was okay with it. I went to the congregation that night and ... I said, 'If these men start coming to our church, they'll change the face of our church. And not only will they change the face of our church, they'll change the way the community looks at our church.' Because we're a rural community, small church."[8] The congregants decided to take up the challenge, and for Neal, it became a transformative experience.

"We were prepared for it to change the face of our church," Neal said. "What we weren't prepared for was for it to change the heart of our church ... We were seeing so many of these good men that were just broken by their addiction, and I found myself at a point where I was having a hard time reconciling what I had always believed with what I was now seeing in these men, and I struggled with that for a little while."[9]

Inspired by what he experienced in his own congregation, Neal boned up on addiction and became the legislature's leading advocate on the issue. That led to an invitation from Pew to a conference about justice reinvestment. The meeting was bipartisan, but the pitch was in line with Pew's focus on bringing around conservatives: speakers included Jerry Madden, the Texas legislator, and Bill MacInturff, a noted Republican pollster. Neal grew determined to bring the JRI model to Georgia and persuaded the Republican House Speaker, David Ralston, to appoint him as chair of the committee that oversees state prisons, even though Neal had never served on it before.[10]

Shortly after Deal's election, Neal visited the governor to introduce his ideas and ask him to sign on to a formal letter asking for Pew's assistance. "I don't know if I got more than a sentence or two out and he started talking about what he wanted to do with criminal justice reform, and it was just like he'd been in every meeting that we'd been having," Neal said. "He was on the same page with everything."[11]

Pew quietly helped to lay the groundwork for action in Georgia in other ways, too. A Right on Crime event mobilized the Georgia Public Policy Foundation, the state's leading conservative think tank, to join the effort. In 2009, GPPF head Kelly McCutchen saw Marc Levin and Jerry Madden tell their story at an event in Washington. Future Right on Crime signatory Edwin Meese was also there. "It really got my attention," McCutchen recalls. "I said, 'Oh gosh, Ed Meese is saying this. This is interesting.'"[12] In December 2010, GPPF hosted a major legislative forum that spotlighted the issue of justice reform. Madden and Levin spoke in a session moderated by Pew's Adam Gelb, who lives in Georgia and led the Georgia Sentencing Commission before coming to work for the foundation.

The Deal–Neal venture in Georgia was just as unlikely as Jerry Madden's efforts in Texas. Georgia may be less notorious than Texas in the national consciousness, but it has long been a cradle of tough-on-crime politics. In 1994, Gov. Zell Miller—a conservative Democrat—ushered in one of the nation's harshest mandatory-sentencing regimes, which covered seven crimes that became known as the "Seven Deadly Sins," all of which led to life without parole after just two convictions.[13] For good measure, the state mandated that juveniles accused of these crimes be tried and sentenced as adults. And Pew found that Georgia's 1-in-13 rate of people under correctional control was the highest in the country in 2009.[14] As the Democratic House minority leader, Stacey Abrams, put it: "This is not an environment that would usually be conducive to a discussion of lessening penalties, improving reentry, and keeping people out of jail. That is not a traditional conversation [to have] in the South."[15]

Nathan Deal's own political biography, however, provides a clue as to how the opening for that discussion was created in Georgia. Deal was first elected to Congress as a conservative Democrat. But after the Gingrich revolution of 1994, he shifted his allegiances and became a Republican. In 2002, Republicans took control of the Georgia Senate for the first time since Reconstruction; the House of Representatives followed two years later.[16] In 2010, the year that Deal was elected governor, Republicans swept all statewide offices in Georgia for the first time since Reconstruction and came within one seat of a legislative supermajority.[17] Just as in Texas, partisan realignment reduced the incentive for members of either party to grandstand on the crime issue. And it meant that Republicans now owned the problem—lock, stock, and barrel.

CONVERSION AT THE CAPITOL

By early 2011, Nathan Deal had made clear that criminal-justice reform was going to be a signature issue of his first term. In fact, it was the first policy item he covered in his inaugural speech.[18] That political commitment by a newly elected governor made it almost impossible for other GOP leaders to stand in the way. "There was the aspect [of] this is a new governor and he's taking the lead on this, and he's the governor of our party, and we're going to get behind him," Worthy said.[19]

Georgia submitted a formal request to Pew for assistance with the project, and then state leaders set about following what has become the procedural template for JRI. In the 2011 legislative session, the Georgia General Assembly voted to establish a bipartisan, interbranch commission that would study the justice system, with Pew handling the analytic grunt work and then make recommendations. These commissions are a staple of the Pew/CSG approach to justice reinvestment. By operating on the assumption that final recommendations will reflect a consensus of the commission, they establish a cooperative tone from the start. Thompson had argued in one of his earliest strategy papers that including traditionally punitive constituencies, such as victim groups and law enforcement, was essential for any JRI program to work: "The value of consulting crime victims, their advocates, and other key stakeholders before modifying sentencing laws and release policies cannot be understated and should be obvious—especially to elected officials who learned their lesson the hard way in the 1980s and 1990s."[20]

The consensual approach is also essential for CSG and Pew to maintain their nonpartisan, technocratic bona fides. Critics say it has the effect of cutting out advocates for the communities most affected by the prison system, making the process less representative and ultimately less sustainable. But backers argue that the lower-profile setting, the long lead time, and the staff support that come with the commission approach are necessary to detoxify the politics of crime, and that grassroots voices often are not organized enough to bring to the table.[21]

The Georgia commission included representatives of law enforcement, ensuring skeptics would be in on the negotiations from the start. Deal made clear he wanted criminal-justice insiders on his team: "If you can convince the people who are working in the system that there is a better way," he said, "they are in a much more influential position to convince the general public that something needs to be done, rather than someone from the outside trying to take that on alone." Deal was not just picking off moderates, either. Prosecutors were represented by David McDade, a district attorney who made national news in 2007 for his aggressive pursuit of a 17-year-old boy who had consensual oral sex with a 15-year-old girl at a party. McDade not only won a 10-year prison sentence for the elder teen; he distributed tapes of the original incident.[22] "The governor put him on there," Worthy explained, "because he said, you know, if McDade can agree to it, we're not gonna get bit on the ankles when we start the legislative process."[23]

Meetings featured presentations from Pew about what was driving up the state's prison population and what might be done about it. As commission members batted around the proposals, Worthy said, Pew's analysts developed a sense of what would be politically possible. Even so, the commission was unable to avoid all controversy. McDade dissented publicly from a recommendation of "presumptive probation" for low-level drug offenders, which would have tilted the law to discourage prison sentences.[24]

The commission's recommendations were funneled to a special joint committee of the House and Senate. That legislative committee included the lawmakers who had sat on the commission. Because of their months of exposure to the Pew data, Abrams said, she and the other lawmakers were able to provide "internal translation services" for their colleagues, putting the ideas behind the package in plain language. Repeated exposure to the objections of law enforcement at the commission stage also had the benefit of preparing the legislator commissioners to confront such arguments at the legislative stage.[25]

The handoff from commission to legislature was hardly seamless. Rich Golick, the chairman of the House Judiciary Committee, who by law was charged with introducing the bill, had not been a member of the original commission. He acknowledges that he went into the process with a degree of skepticism. "It was very new, very different," Golick said. "And a lot of us, including myself, had a very steep learning curve in a very short amount of time."[26]

The bill that Golick first introduced was distant enough from the commission recommendations to draw a rebuke from the governor's office. A Deal spokesman declared the legislation flawed and said it could actually raise justice costs.[27] At the time, Golick maintained that the bill would avoid "radical, too-fast changes" and would "not sacrifice one inch on public safety," implying that the commission had gone too far.[28] Meanwhile, the Deal team let it be known that it would consider floating a rival bill if Golick's original work was not amended.[29]

But Golick said his views evolved as the session went on. "I was learning as I went," he said. "What turned it for me was really when I had got my head around the data." The numbers, he said, made it impossible to deny something had to change: "Ultimately you really couldn't defeat the reality of the fact that as it related to non-violent drug offenders, the system just wasn't working. It was failing the public in terms of public safety. Why? Because these addicts, these potentially non-violent addicts ... were taking up bed space that should be occupied by violent criminals."[30]

The final legislation was projected to flatline Georgia's prison population, eliminating an increase of 3,200 inmates that had previously been forecast for the coming five years. That would save the state $264 million on the cost of incarceration, according to Pew. For key categories of crimes—burglary, forgery, and drug possession—the legislation created penalty scales so that less-severe offenses would draw lower sentences. The bill also made probation more flexible by authorizing electronic monitoring and allowing officers to impose punishments short of prison without having to go back to a judge. Meanwhile, the state spent $35.2 million to add 600 drug-treatment beds for incarcerated offenders and steered $11.6 million into accountability courts like the one run by Nathan Deal's son.[31] Even though Deal considered the final package a victory, it left out some important recommendations the council had offered, such as "presumptive probation" and a so-called safety valve to mandatory-minimum drug sentences.[32]

Pew put significant firepower behind the package. The foundation commissioned a poll showing that 85 percent of Georgians agreed with the principles of the legislation and hired both a public-relations shop and a lobbying firm to promote the measure.[33] The Right on Crime alliance also swung into action, with Newt Gingrich penning a supportive op-ed and the Georgia Public Policy Foundation compiling a state-level version of the "statement of principles," signed by prominent Georgians.[34] Meanwhile, Prison Fellowship worked with its volunteers in Georgia to identify pastors who could approach one or two particularly skeptical lawmakers.[35]

Abrams said such endorsements, and the specter of Texas, were never far from the conversation. "I cannot remember a single time when it was talked about when those examples weren't used," she said. "Again, no one likes to be first when it comes to trying something that is not easy. And having other states not only try it but succeed created the space for Georgia to hear them and I think created the space for conservatives to get beyond what I think could be a knee-jerk reaction."[36] Indeed, reform backers stressed the Texas example in their public rhetoric. A judge who was on the commission said, "We don't have to reinvent the wheel. We have seen similar reform efforts enacted in some very conservative states, which have seen significant cost savings and maintained public safety."[37]

Worthy downplayed the role of such outside examples. "I don't think that was a big part of it down here," he said. "[Legislators] weren't calling D.C. or calling Austin, Texas. They were calling Waycross, Georgia, saying, 'Hey, sheriff.'" In fact, it was important that policymakers had access to data analysis customized to Georgia, Worthy said, as opposed to being asked to adopt one-size-fits-all solutions.[38] But a comment by Golick highlights the importance of opening policymakers to data in the first place: "When you've got a really 'soft-on-crime' state like Texas coming forward with reforms like this," he said with an ironic chuckle, "that's something that you have no choice—especially in a deeply red state like ours—to take notice of. But ultimately, I think it was really a combination of factors. It was the governor's seriousness about it. It was the fact that we had seen and heard about this in other states that were politically in alignment with Georgia. And then I think the third leg of that stool, really just for me personally, was ultimately really the data."[39]

Still, endorsements, data, and persuasion did not do the job alone. Worthy observed, "Screaming matches were had. Certain House members had to be told that they were gonna get run over by the governor's train if they, you know, didn't get on board."[40] Meanwhile, Golick said police and DAs were not fully persuaded in that first year. "While we all, certainly in this state, have a deep respect for law enforcement and the job that they do, you know, they're a bloc, a bureaucracy as well, and they'll go ahead and be resistant to change as much as any other," Golick said. But, he said, "I think sometimes in the legislative process an interested party will simply come to the conclusion that 'This is happening,' and it's better to go ahead and put your thumbprint [on it], you know, have as much as effect [as possible] on something that you ultimately don't like because it's going to pass anyway, so you might as well be at the table and be a good-faith partner in it."[41]

For prosecutors, who were accustomed to wielding almost unquestioned authority over all things law and order in Georgia, being cast as an inflexible bureaucracy by their usual Republican allies and losing control of the political agenda represented an unwelcome reversal of fortune. The aura of inevitability that surrounded Deal's proposals, while driven by the governor's own investment of political capital, was enhanced by a stream of conservative endorsements and the frequent reference to the Texas precedent. Chuck Spahos, executive director of the Prosecuting Attorneys Council of Georgia, expressed a sense of resignation about such greater forces at work in a 2013 conversation. Asked about a just-passed reform of juvenile justice, designed as a follow-up to the adult reforms of 2012, Spahos said, "We really haven't had a conversation with the legislature about that. They told us this is what we're going to do, and they've moved down the road." Pressed on whether prosecutors were consulted, he added, "I don't at all mean to say that we were not very involved in this conversation. It's just . . . a national trend that we're going to take a different approach, and it's not my job to get up there and persuade them what we should or shouldn't be doing. I can point things out and they make those decisions." In reference to a modest mandatory-minimum sentencing reform, also passed that year, Spahos remarked, "What they think is we spend too much money on corrections. And it's no longer popular to do so." Spahos's downbeat tone suggests that prosecutors perceived reform as an overwhelming force, and that they were now in a mode of reacting to, rather than driving, the politics of criminal justice in the state.[42]

The arguments were sealed with an impressive result: the final bill cleared the legislature without a single dissenting vote. It was an outcome consistent with Pew's general strategy of garnering support by overwhelming majorities, even if it means limiting the scope of initial reforms. As of April 2015, legislation backed by the Pew/CSG/Vera triumvirate in all the states had accumulated more than 5,700 supportive votes and fewer than 500 nays, a difference of more than 10 to 1.[43]

Could more have been achieved if Pew and its allies in the states were willing to win by smaller margins? Abrams, the Georgia Democrat, said it was critical to keep an overwhelming majority of legislators behind the bill, especially Republicans, who dominate the state's General Assembly. "You want the party in power to make the choices because then they take responsibility for those choices," she said. Having a majority of Republicans backing the legislation would strengthen the governor's case and make it more likely that other measures required to fully implement the program, like funding for alternatives to incarceration, would also survive, she said.[44] Most significantly, the vote committed the state's Republican Party squarely to a redirection of criminal justice, one that would have significance for the later trajectory of policymaking.

At the same time, Jay Neal praised Abrams for ensuring her caucus got behind the reforms, even if they did not go far enough for many Democrats. "It's an easy thing for the minority party to vote no to a bill that they want to see passed just so they can say they voted no because it didn't go far enough. She did a good job of helping them understand where we were going, not just that we were having a vote on one bill, but that there was a real effort to change the way Georgia had done things over the course of the last couple of decades."[45] Gambling on Republicans to change the culture of criminal justice in Georgia may just be paying off.

MOMENTUM—AND LIMITS

The 2012 effort has set off a virtuous cycle of reform in Georgia. State leaders are quick to insist they have not gone soft, but they have opened up space on an issue that previously seemed impenetrable. It has become easy for politicians to talk about and vote for successive waves of criminal-justice reform. While none of these bills taken individually are as revolutionary as some national advocates would hope for, when viewed as a whole they represent a clear change in policy direction.

The circle of state leaders who are passionate about the cause has broadened beyond Deal and Neal. The suspicions of law enforcement have been eased, but their monopoly on expertise when it comes to crime has also been successfully toppled. The blue-ribbon commission model has been institutionalized and widely accepted as a way to make crime policy decisions. New agencies have been created to implement the reforms, creating further institutional support for the cause. And increasingly, the reforms have come to be politically rewarding, attracting national attention as a feel-good success story.

Not long after he signed that first bill, the governor called his study commission back to order, with a new charge, revamping Georgia's juvenile-justice system. Here, too, there was a precedent: Texas followed its adult reforms with an overhaul of juvenile justice. The commission recommended reforms that, over five years, were projected to cut juvenile incarceration one-third below the baseline and save $85 million.[46] Georgia legislators approved most of the package in 2013 with no opposing votes.[47] They also approved a version of the mandatory-minimum reforms that had been left out of the original bill.[48] But Deal was not done: he put the commission back to work again, and in 2014 it delivered a series of recommendations on how to improve reentry programming for ex-cons returning to their communities, and the bill based on that passed nearly unanimously as well.[49] As he began his second term, in 2015, Deal kept at it. He signed an executive order banning most state agencies from asking about prior felonies on job applications.[50] He pushed through new funding for in-prison education, and won unanimous support for legislation to rein in abusive practices by private companies that handle some probationers and to create a new Department of Community Supervision to manage probation and parole statewide.[51]

The commission has also matured. In 2013, legislators decided to continue it for at least another five years, with commissioners serving that entire period so they could develop expertise.[52] The incremental, consensual strategy has changed the policymaking environment drastically since 2012, commissioners said. "I'm knocking on wood as I say this, [but] the General Assembly has such confidence and faith in the fairness of the council's work, in the processes by which they do their work, that usually legislative adoption has basically become perfunctory," Worthy said.[53] Indeed, the *Atlanta Journal-Constitution* observed that Deal's reentry legislation in 2014 "encountered minimal resistance and gained almost no attention despite being the final part of fundamental changes in the state's approach to criminals."[54] Abrams said Georgia policymakers have developed the capacity "to believe that this is true and that this works. And that came about because we were slower."[55]

Georgia dedicated more than $48 million to adult and juvenile justice reforms in its 2013–2015 budget period, and Golick said the legislature is committed to continuing that support.[56] "We've come this far on it," he said. "It would just be dumb to just let it go. That would not make sense. And it would actually be fiscally irresponsible."[57] Other legislators echo that logic. When Deal in 2015 sought additional justice-reform funding, the chairman of Georgia's House Appropriations Committee said that he had heard no objections. "Members have seen the difference that it's made in the lives of the inmates," Rep. Terry England said.[58]

They've also seen a difference in the numbers. Georgia's prison population in 2014 was 3 percent smaller than five years earlier. Much larger declines were registered in new admissions to prison, which sank almost 15 percent, driven by a 20 percent drop in admissions of black offenders.[59] As a result, the amount that Georgia pays local county jails to house state prisoners has dropped by some $20 million in recent budgets.[60]

Meanwhile, Georgia, and its governor, are collecting national accolades that cannot help but encourage the trend. The Marshall Project has admiringly called Georgia "the laboratory of criminal-justice reform."[61] Deal was a featured speaker at a heavily promoted "Bipartisan Summit on Criminal Justice Reform" in 2014 that included all the Right on Crime heavyweights and liberal activist Van Jones.[62]

The reform could have easily turned sour if a supporter had paid for it electorally. But Worthy said the governor's office closely monitored the state legislative elections that followed the first reform and found that not a single incumbent was attacked for being soft on crime.[63] Since then, Deal has turned the issue, which he initially described as a potential political liability, into a major asset.[64] He touted his justice reforms on the campaign trail, and it was the rare issue on which his opponent, Jimmy Carter's grandson, did not criticize him.[65] Deal even used the issue to seek votes from black voters, who are overwhelmingly Democratic. A dozen black ministers endorsed him at a joint appearance late in the campaign.[66] Democratic politicians should take note, Abrams said: "If you do the work that fundamentally transforms lives, that's going to matter."[67]

Jay Neal can agree with that. The pastor-turned-legislator gave up his seat in the Georgia House in 2013 for a full-time job institutionalizing the state's new path. Governor Deal appointed him to be the first executive director of a newly created Office of Reentry and Transition Services, where he started work on a five-year plan to design state-of-the-art reentry services for the more than 25,000 Georgians who leave state prison every year.

Neal says this cause was always bigger to him than the legislative seat. Early in the process, a friend warned him to stay away from the justice-reform issue, but he ignored that advice: "I could have just went with the flow and been elected over and over again, and not accomplished anything, and I wouldn't have felt like I was successful. But if I do what I felt like God placed me there to do, and I helped change the culture of Georgia, and somebody somewhere down the road spends a lot of money and convinces voters that I've been soft on crime and I've had the shorter political career than I otherwise would have—then I'm okay with that."[68]

One key plank of Georgia's new reentry plan involves getting churches more involved in mentoring inmates as they return to society.[69] It's the type of idea that makes many liberals queasy, but building on the interest of evangelicals could pay real political returns if it deepens their engagement and makes them more likely to support subsequent reforms.

For all the momentum Georgia leaders have summoned behind justice reform, however, they have largely shied away from tackling one of the key drivers of prison growth: unnecessarily long sentences for violent criminals. For many conservative reformers, the distinction between nonviolent and violent offenders remains sacrosanct. Golick said the idea that prison beds should be saved for the incarceration of violent offenders was fundamental to the pitch he and others made to the Georgia legislature in passing the 2012 package. "What I think really turned the legislature—and this was really not me, it was Governor Deal, I was just the messenger—[was] that it really had to do with breaking apart that violent v. nonviolent [offender]."

Indeed, Deal has repeatedly stressed the distinction in his public remarks. "By identifying low-risk, nonviolent offenders and more effective ways to rehabilitate them, we are steering these offenders away from a life of crime and reserving our expensive prison beds for the violent offenders who pose a public safety risk," Deal said when he signed the 2012 legislation.[70] That notion of conserving prison space to focus on violent offenders has been supplemented with some blustery rhetoric. In his inaugural speech, Deal declared: "For violent and repeat offenders, we will make you pay for your crimes."[71]

In an interview, the governor explained that his insistence on the nonviolent/violent distinction was both pragmatic and principled. "You cannot undertake criminal justice reform if you leave the public with the impression that you're going to make them less safe. If they ever have that idea, you will not be successful with the reform."

Referring to sex offenders and violent offenders, Deal added: "I believe those are generally the kind of people that do need to be kept away from society, because they do pose a danger to our society." Pressed on whether he could imagine a future where long sentences for violent offenders might be scaled back, Deal said: "I think so, but that is something that I think we have to give the confidence to the judges that . . . they're not going to see someone that does pose a danger to their community—that we're not going to see them just simply turned back on the street very quickly." Instead, Deal said, judges must believe that offenders will acquire new skills in prison that allow them to succeed on the outside. If Georgia can build effective in-prison services, Deal said, a judge can impose a shorter sentence with the confidence that "that early-released individual is going to be much less likely of committing another offense than this person who served a long sentence but has not had anything adjusted about them from the time they first went in. I think that is the kind of transition we're going to seek to happen in our state."

Worthy also encouraged a patient approach to the question of lengthy prison sentences. "I think that it's called a political process for a reason. And I think that whenever there is a complex issue that has a great deal of emotional aspects attached to it, I think it is a process. It is not a philosopher-king waves a magic wand and makes all of the changes overnight. And I think that success should be judged on whether or not the process has continued, and whether or not the process has continued in a substantive manner."[72]

That patience remains packaged with fiery rhetoric about violent offenders being "put away," however, posing a real danger that reformers will be unable to roll back sentences for violent offenses even where it is safe—and sensible—to do so.[73] Meanwhile, prosecutors have not exactly raised the white flag. Danny Porter, the district attorney for Gwinnett County, said prosecutors were able to extract significant concessions in the juvenile justice reforms, and more recently were able to limit the reach of a measure allowing some drug offenders to win retroactive release from life sentences imposed under recidivist statutes. Porter said he was comfortable with much of Deal's agenda, but added that the state may be nearing the limit of what's reasonable: "I think we're at the point where we're scraping the bottom of the barrel looking for people to get out of prison," he said.[74]

FOLLOW THE LEADER

It is a common myth that Georgia was founded as a British penal colony. In fact, the vision of founder James Oglethorpe was quite the opposite. His aim was to create a safe haven for people swept up in Britain's infamous debtor's prisons. Far from shipping hardened criminals to serve out their sentences in the New World, he wanted to create a society that no longer punished poverty.[75]

The realities of colonization were, unsurprisingly, quite different. But Georgia may now be picking up the pieces of Oglethorpe's vision, and dispelling preconceived notions about what its justice system stands for. In fact, just as Texas was touted as a model for Georgia, the Peach State increasingly is being pitched as an example for others to follow. Pew has invited Worthy, Neal, and others to speak about the Georgia experience at forums around the country, in Alabama, Colorado, Florida, Mississippi, Oregon, and Washington, D.C., Deal says the governor's office has also fielded inquiries from his counterparts in other states.[76]

Table 8.1 Select sentencing reforms in GOP-controlled states

State	Year	Projected Impact/ Highlights*	Conservative Support
Mississippi[77]	2014	Savings of 3,460 prison beds over 10 years, and an actual reduction of 1,500; confirms major rollback of truth-in-sentencing passed in 2008; establishes flexible penalties for parole violations; lowers sentences for minor drug and theft offenses.	Endorsed by Gov. Phil Bryant; passed with Republican majorities in both chambers. Previous reforms endorsed by Gov. Haley Barbour.
Ohio[78]	2011	Savings of $46 million over four years; aligns crack/powder penalties; prohibits prison sentences for some low-level felons; expands ability to earn credits toward early release.	Endorsed by Gov. John Kasich; passed with Republican majorities in both chambers.
North Carolina[79]	2011	Savings up to $70 million and 3,100 prison beds over a four year period. Requires all felons to be supervised upon release; limits conditions under which probationers can be sent to prison and allows flexible penalties for violations; expands drug diversion.	Near-unanimous passage in the GOP-controlled legislature.
South Carolina[80]	2010	Savings of 1,786 prison beds and $400 million over five years; aligns crack/powder penalties; requires risk assessments; increases violent-crime penalties, but cuts others.	Endorsed by Gov. Mark Sanford; 14 Republican cosponsors.

* *Impact estimates are as reported at time of passage.*

Georgia is hardly alone in following the Texas precedent. Table 8.1 illustrates how other conservative-controlled states have approved laws explicitly designed to imprison fewer offenders.

To be sure, reforms such as these typically make only modest dents in a huge problem of over-incarceration. Prison beds "saved" are often merely beds that will not have to be built in the future, rather than actual reductions. But it remains the case that "justice reinvestment" laws are advertised publicly for their effect on *reducing* imprisonment, not embedding it. At the very least, then, these packages represent a fundamental shift in the definition of the problem. Moreover, as the Texas and Georgia cases suggest, an initial round of relatively modest reforms can generate momentum for more. Such reforms put conservative politicians on record in support of something other than increasing punitiveness, put supporters of the status quo on the back foot, establish reducing recidivism as a long-term agenda item in the state, and provide an opportunity for Republicans to look deeply at the evidence on mass incarceration. In all these ways, they have the potential to make the next step, and the step after that, easier.

Mississippi, for example, has also shown that the reform appetite can grow with the eating. With Keene's friend Haley Barbour in the governor's mansion, Mississippi in 2009 cut the time that nonviolent offenders were required to serve on their prison sentences from 85 percent to a mere 25 percent, and promptly paroled more than 3,000 of them in a six-month period.[81] By 2011, however, the prison population began to grow again.[82] So in 2014, lawmakers went further, approving a package of reforms that was predicted to keep the inmate count flat for the next decade, saving $266 million.[83]

Parsing out the contribution of the identity vouchers at Right on Crime and ALEC to all this change is a difficult task. Politicians may not recognize how much such precedents shape their decisions. Or they may be loath to admit it, preferring to cast themselves as independent thinkers. On the other hand, they may find it in their interest to heap praise on national figures with whom they expect future interactions. But leaders in Mississippi said it mattered there. Lieutenant Governor Tate Reeves explained: "It's helpful when David Keene, it's helpful when Speaker Gingrich, it's helpful when ALEC is on board ... My role is to make sure we have the votes on the floor of the Senate to get this passed. And I will tell you this particular group [Right on Crime], and the strength that you bring to the process, really mattered."[84] Republican Senator Brice Wiggins recalled being approached by a Tea Party legislator who wondered if the proposed legislation was soft. Wiggins said he told the legislator about Right on Crime and named prominent conservatives who were backing justice reforms. "Once they heard that," he said, "it was sold."[85]

Meanwhile, the accumulation of reforms across states may be creating a self-reinforcing cycle. With each state that acts, others feel more pressure to follow suit. "How many times has a Louisianian claimed their state can never be the most backward in the union so long as the great state of Mississippi's around?," an op-ed writer asked in the *New Orleans Times-Picayune*, before warning that Mississippi's justice reform was putting that claim into question.[86] That's even though Louisiana leaders had already made some politically tough choices, allowing the waiver of mandatory-minimum sentences, limited sanctions for probation violations, and reducing some truth-in-sentencing requirements. In 2014, they expanded the option to waive mandatory minimums to some violent offenses.[87]

Less colorfully, but perhaps just as effectively, Florida reformers repeatedly turn to the example of their neighbor to the north to urge changes in Tallahassee. For example, leaders of the Project on Accountable Justice at Florida State University said they worked intensively with journalists at the conservative Jacksonville-based *Florida Times-Union* to bring about a three-part series of editorials advocating reform, touting Georgia as the model. "States like Georgia and Texas have shown the way forward," the newspaper declared. "It's time for Florida to catch up."[88]

It's not just laggard states that are feeling pressure to play "catch-up" to places like Georgia and Texas, however. The momentum generated in state capitals has now swept into the nation's criminal-justice reform laggard—the federal government.

CHAPTER 9

Trickle-Up Reform

In 1995, as Pat Nolan neared the end of his confinement, the U.S. Sentencing Commission was gearing up to eliminate the 100-to-1 disparity in federal sentences for crimes involving crack and powder cocaine. That decision could still have been overturned by Congress, however. So Nolan put his telephone privileges at the prison to work and lobbied lawmakers from behind bars. He managed to line up commitments from Republican members of Congress to stand by the commission. But a few days after commissioners officially voted, then–Attorney General Janet Reno announced her opposition to equalizing the penalties, and the Republicans Nolan had won over reneged.[1] "We can't let the Democrats get to our right on crime," he recalls being told.[2] It was a brutal lesson: even where the injustices were so extreme that both sides could see them, the white-hot politics of crime in the 1990s made reform at the federal level all but impossible.

Twenty years later, the whole definition of letting someone "get to your right" on crime has been upended. Congress has passed laws to protect prisoners against sexual abuse and to help them transition successfully into the "real world" upon their release. The infamous crack/powder disparity has been eased, if not equalized. By late 2015, even serious reform of mandatory-minimum sentences was on the table.

These breakthroughs resulted from a mix of structural changes and identity-vouching efforts similar to that which drove reforms in the states. As chapter 3 showed, declining rates of victimization combined with the rise of terrorism to knock street crime from the agenda in Congress. The 2010 election was a crucial moment of generational change, sweeping into office Tea Party–affiliated lawmakers who redoubled conservative skepticism of government and did not carry the baggage of the "tough-on-crime" 1980s and 1990s.

Meanwhile, Nolan and his growing network worked assiduously to persuade other national conservatives that criminal justice was worth a second look. For years, the primary way Nolan's associates supported him was by advising on, endorsing, or actively lobbying for bills in Congress. They operated incrementally and strategically, picking battles that could be framed in terms attractive to conservatives, such as religious freedom, spiritual redemption, and government overreach. These arguments could only work if they were delivered by credible, conservative messengers, the list of which grew with each round in the legislative campaign. Some of them offered public endorsements, some lobbied politicians directly, and some merely let it be known privately that they were "behind" an idea. Gradually, these efforts established the sense that criminal-justice reform was a conservative cause. The surge of reform in conservative states was an important ingredient in this process, creating a new group of red-state legislators who could vouch for the right-wing bona fides of the cause.

THE LEAST OF THESE

The first wave of conservative reform successes occurred primarily through a moral framing that appealed to religious conservatives. The clearest route to reach these believers was the issue of prisoners' religious rights. The claim that prisoners were being denied freedom of worship was consistent with social conservatives' argument that religion was under assault by a growing secular state. In 1997, Nolan fought a proposal by Senator Harry Reid of Nevada that would have made prisoners ineligible for the protections of the Religious Freedom Restoration Act (RFRA), a 1992 law that had given plaintiffs a wide berth to challenge state and federal laws on the grounds that they violated religious freedom.[3] Reid's initiative floundered amid opposition not only from Republican Senators Dan Coats of Indiana (who had previously hired Colson protégé Michael Gerson as a senior staffer) and John Ashcroft of Missouri, but also Democrat Ted Kennedy of Massachusetts.[4] Those senators stood in rare opposition to state attorneys general, who had lined up behind Reid, irritated as they were by lawsuits such as one from a prisoner who claimed fealty to the Church of Filet Mignon.[5] The issue soon came roaring back onto the agenda, however, when the Supreme Court ruled that RFRA could not apply to the states, but only the federal government.[6] In the wake of the decision, Colson led a coalition of top evangelical leaders who circulated a statement denouncing what they saw as an epidemic of antireligious judicial activism.[7] Congress soon passed a narrower law designed to restore some of what the Supreme Court had chipped away. Protection of prisoners' rights loomed large in these deliberations, and Prison Fellowship was the leading voice on the issue, with Nolan and his boss, Colson, both testifying before Congress.[8] Other evangelicals rallied behind them: Jim Dobson's Focus on the Family backed Nolan and Colson against Reid, and in the wake of the Supreme Court decision, Dobson was joined by the Family Research Council, Southern Baptist Convention, Christian Coalition, and National Association of Evangelicals.[9]

Prison Fellowship now had a clear position of legislative leadership among conservative Christians, and beginning in 2002 it deepened that claim when it joined a campaign to curb the sexual abuse of prisoners. The effort was led by Michael Horowitz, a longtime conservative strategist based at the Hudson Institute. Horowitz had played a major role in building the movement's legal infrastructure in the 1980s and later became a key coalition builder on issues of international human rights, especially those with a religious dimension.[10] He was now advocating what he called the "Wilberforce Agenda," designed to rally religious conservatives around clear-cut moral causes that would undermine perceptions they were uncaring and focused only on issues of sexual propriety.[11] As part of this effort, Horowitz assembled a coalition of left and right to push for legislation that would reduce the incidence of rape in American prisons.

The struggle for what would become the Prison Rape Elimination Act marked the evangelical movement's first major claim to influence over prison policy. The law was endorsed by the same slate of evangelical groups that backed Colson on RFRA (joined by a handful of others).[12] It was championed in the House by Virginia Rep. Frank Wolf, a noted religious conservative and supporter of international human rights. Wolf, who has called Colson "a dear friend, mentor and brother," said he pushed the bill after Colson approached him about it.[13] Alabama Republican Jeff Sessions cosponsored the measure in the Senate, and his commitment also carried the fingerprints of Prison

Fellowship. Sessions's office often consulted with then–
Alabama Attorney General Bill Pryor on matters of justice
policy. In turn, Pryor had worked with Prison Fellowship
on the bill, according to a statement Sessions made on the
floor. "Chuck Colson with Prison Fellowship was a leader
that conservatives, like Senator Sessions, respected," former Sessions aide Ed Haden reflected. "Colson had been
to prison, changed his life on a religious basis, and worked
with a ministry that helped prisoners across the country.
He knew what issues prisoners were facing. He spoke with
authority . . . We believed that Chuck Colson's and General
Pryor's support would help get votes on the Senate floor.
It did."[14] Colson's influence on Wolf and Sessions aside,
Prison Fellowship was an important deputy to Horowitz
in the anti-rape effort, working the phones and mobilizing
supporters.[15] The measure passed both houses of Congress
unanimously in 2003, over the deep reservations of the
Bush Justice Department.

On the heels of this success, Prison Fellowship found
a new opportunity to plant the evangelical flag on prison
policy and move fully into the role of lead legislative strategist. Nolan had become friends with Gene Guerrero,
an official who worked on criminal-justice issues in the
Washington office of the Open Society Foundations, the
same liberal foundation that got "justice reinvestment"
started. Guerrero led a coalition of liberals that had been
working with a Democratic congressman, Danny Davis,
on legislation to help released prisoners successfully reinte-
grate into society, and Nolan joined the effort as the lone
conservative advocate.

Meanwhile, similar ideas were germinating on the
Republican side, driven by the "compassionate conserva-
tive" agenda of George W. Bush. To run his new Office of
Faith-Based Programs, the president had hired the political

scientist John DiIulio, a friend of Colson's who over the course of the 1990s had gone from advocating for more prisons to declaring that incarceration had gotten out of hand.[16] In 2001, DiIulio pushed the administration to launch a $150 million program aimed at reducing recidivism among serious and violent offenders.[17] Three years later, the president called in his State of the Union address for legislation to assist ex-offenders with reentry, a product of his ongoing conversations about the issue with administration officials.

Meanwhile, Davis's work on reentry legislation had already been joined by Ohio Republican Congressman Rob Portman, a supporter of the "compassionate conservative" agenda who had a longtime interest in drug policy and close links to the White House. The initiative had the potential to become a rare bipartisan victory, and Guerrero and Nolan were in the thick of the negotiations to make it happen. "I talked to Gene Guerrero and Pat Nolan every day for five years," recalled Jessica Nickel, who was Portman's lead staffer on what became known as the Second Chance Act. Prison Fellowship focused on recruiting Republican support in Congress.[18] On the Senate side, the bill was cosponsored by Senator Sam Brownback, a longtime friend of the organization.[19] Prison Fellowship also took the lead in soliciting evangelical endorsements, once again bringing along the Southern Baptist Convention, National Association of Evangelicals, and the Family Research Council.[20] For good measure, Nolan's friend Keene solicited the endorsement of the American Conservative Union, where he was chairman.[21]

The battle for the Second Chance Act of 2008 took five years, as the advocates slogged through disputes over the role of faith organizations, federalism concerns, and sheer inertia. But the long process had an upside. It allowed a genuine working relationship between left- and right-wing reformers to develop, based on the understanding that each side was coming to the table for its own reasons. Just as importantly, Nickel said, it changed the tone of crime policymaking in Congress. "I think it brought both sides together to work on the criminal justice issue in a safe way that was based on evidence and science," Nickel said. "You saw people come together to want to do it the right way, and it was no longer sort of the easy, knee-jerk criminal-justice politics [of] the old guard."[22]

In the decade after he joined Prison Fellowship, Nolan and his network made significant progress on justice reform in Washington against long odds. They did so by deploying the power of reputation—winning the endorsements of evangelical groups and prominent conservatives—and by framing their case in terms that would resonate with conservative ideology. Their legislative agenda, emphasizing themes such as the humanity of the imprisoned and the possibility of redemption, proved compelling to key professionals and politicians on the Hill. A vivid example comes from Ed Haden, the Sessions staffer who worked on the Prison Rape Elimination Act. Most Senate Judiciary Committee staffers were indifferent to the issue until they attended a hearing on the proposed legislation, Haden said. The mother of a rape victim who had committed suicide testified about her story. "After they saw that," Haden said, "they went from, 'Who gives a crap about this bill,' to 'Okay, we're down.'"[23]

This was not the product of a master plan. Nolan's strategy developed ad hoc, as he seized on opportunities created by other players—Horowitz in the case of PREA, and Portman, Davis, and the liberals around Guerrero in the case of Second Chance. The White House's "compassionate conservative" agenda also provided Nolan with an early boost (though it soon petered out). Moreover, Nickel says there was already plenty of commitment among the Hill staffers who drove the Second Chance Act, many of whom had personal reasons to care about the criminal-justice system, from a professional background to a family tragedy.[24]

Still, Nolan and his network created a consistency and thematic coherence that otherwise would not have existed, and contributed substantially to the success of PREA and Second Chance. These victories allowed them to crack the taboo on criticizing law enforcement and prisons and to put at least a few Republicans on record as supporting some reform. Inside Congress, they cultivated a group of lawmakers and staff who would play important roles in subsequent, deeper reforms. PREA champion Wolf would sponsor a significant funding boost for justice reinvestment, as described in chapter 6. Second Chance Act sponsor Brownback made justice reform and reentry programming a priority after he became governor of Kansas in 2011.[25] Another key player in the Second Chance Act, Wisconsin Congressman Jim Sensenbrenner, would go on to sponsor a sweeping proposal to reform the federal justice system in 2015.

"BUREAUCRATS WITH GUNS"

At the same time that evangelicals were putting a human face on the prison issue, another set of conservatives was stressing a different angle: that criminal justice had become just another playground where out-of-control government officials toyed with citizens' lives and livelihoods.

The first volley in this line of attack came in the 1990s, when Illinois Congressman Henry Hyde took up the battle against abuses of civil asset forfeiture, which allows law enforcement to seize assets alleged to have been used in a crime without convicting the owner. The Illinois

Congressman filed reform legislation in 1993, but it went nowhere. In 1995, Hyde published a book on asset forfeiture with the libertarian Cato Institute. The same year, Hyde became chairman of the House Judiciary Committee and slowly began to get traction on the issue. By 1997, outlets ranging from the *National Review* to the *Wall Street Journal* to the *Washington Times* had published exposés and op-eds claiming that asset forfeiture had gotten out of control, and Hyde found high-powered allies both left and right, including the ACLU and the NRA.[26] In 1999, David Keene issued his own call for reform.[27] The following year, former Reagan confidant Ed Meese conceded that the system midwifed by his administration had become deeply flawed. "It is important for law enforcement leaders not to allow the money to be the tail wagging the dog," Meese said.[28] But Hyde's reform effort faced vociferous opposition from the Justice Department and state and local law enforcement, still fearsome voices. A bill got through Congress in 2000, but by the time of passage it had been watered down enough that, as one critic said, it wouldn't "make a cotton-picking bit of difference."[29] As with the crack/powder issue, even a glaring injustice could not translate into serious congressional action in this era. With outrage building on the one hand and strong interest groups digging in on the other, legislators settled on a familiar solution: accepting reform in principle while gutting it in practice.

Another decade of asset-forfeiture abuses provided additional fodder for advocates to shock conservatives into reevaluating their assumptions about criminal justice, however. The libertarian Institute for Justice had participated in the 1990s reform drive, but in 2010, it put the issue back on the agenda with a report titled *Policing for Profit*.[30] As Scott Bullock, who directs the IJ's work in the area, argues, conservatives got behind arming police with such sweeping power because the laws were passed at the height of the drug war. "That caused folks to set aside some of these usual concerns about the abuse of power that you see and what happens when you give government agencies and officials these sweeping powers that exist under civil forfeiture laws and then set this perverse financial incentive to go out and take as much property as possible." IJ was able, in a way that would be difficult for those on the left, to inject a vigorously anti-statist, antitax frame into this issue, making it more consistent with the rhetoric of the rising Tea Party. "Seeing this voracious appetite for money that was coming from law enforcement ... awakened people to say, 'This isn't about getting the bad guys or solving crimes. This is about raising money for it, and civil forfeiture is a mechanism for them doing so.'" By making the issue about property rights and government abuse, IJ was able to help take the focus off the drug dealers with fancy cars and stacks of money that had justified civil asset forfeiture, and put it onto victims with more sympathy on the right. This work would encourage conservatives to think about the criminal justice system like the rest of government—just "bureaucrats with guns," as a popular phrase among reformers has it.[31]

Meanwhile, a group of conservatives around Meese at the Heritage Foundation was developing an even broader critique of the justice system—and this time the finger was pointed directly at Congress rather than merely at bureaucrats. As described in chapter 4, critics of "over-criminalization" argued that federal criminal law had become far too vague and sweeping, so that overzealous prosecutors could charge virtually anyone with a crime. Congress had become so eager to attach criminal penalties to legislation, and given regulators so much room to define new crimes, that nobody could keep track of them any longer.

As a result, the principle that a perpetrator had to commit his deed with a "guilty mind" was being undermined, said Brian Walsh, a leader of the Heritage effort. This argument had obvious appeal to conservatives when it was illustrated by grotesque prosecutions of small-business owners for regulatory offenses, areas that Meese's group emphasized.[32] In fact, between the early 1980s (when a previous generation of reformers had unsuccessfully campaigned to consolidate the federal criminal code) and the late 2000s, the term "over-criminalization" appeared in congressional documents almost exclusively in a white-collar context.[33]

However, the over-criminalization school also established a connection between overzealous white-collar prosecutions and excesses in street-level enforcement. Intellectually, the claim that Congress had abandoned the "guilty mind" principle was bundled with an argument that even where inherent wrongs were at stake—cases like theft or murder—Congress had asserted too much federal control over state prosecutions. Emotionally, stories about over-the-top prosecutions of businesspeople, schoolchildren, and grandmothers created an "if it happens here" narrative that made conservatives curious about what was happening on the street level. As Walsh put it: "If you could convict a middle manager for criminal negligence and put them in prison, and maybe have no proof that the person actually knew what they were doing was wrongful, it's pretty easy to justify sentencing a low-level drug dealer, or somebody who's a mule, to 20 or 30 years."[34]

Republican mega-donors Charles and David Koch have invoked a similar logic to explain their support for criminal-justice reform. The story the Kochs tell about why they chose to focus on the issue concerns a 1995 criminal prosecution of their company for environmental crimes at a refinery in Corpus Christi. As Koch's chief counsel Mark

Holden explained, "It was a really, really torturous experience ... We learned first-hand what happens when anyone gets into the criminal-justice system." That, Holden said, led Charles Koch to wonder "how the little guy who doesn't have Koch's resources deals with prosecutions like that."[35] No liberal would make a connection between large companies accused of regulatory crimes and low-level drug dealers, but it made complete sense within the world of conservatism, and would provide an increasingly powerful frame to engage those on the right who might not have otherwise thought they had a stake in halting the metastasizing wars on drugs and crime.

In the mid-2000s, Meese's Heritage Foundation began hosting regular meetings on the over-criminalization issue with groups on both left and right. Regular attendees included representatives of the ACLU, Families Against Mandatory Minimums, Institute for Justice, and Washington Legal Foundation, as well as Hill staffers, Walsh said. Pat Nolan was also looped into the effort, and over-criminalization came up frequently at his own, smaller working group of conservatives.[36] Around this time, Heritage also partnered with the National Association of Criminal Defense Lawyers (NACDL), which has a liberal reputation. The group was a fixture at working-group meetings and teamed up with Heritage to ask members of Congress to take on over-criminalization. Walsh recalls that it was slow going at first. "We were getting audibly scoffed at by staffers in some Republican offices on Capitol Hill," he recalls. "And we were getting kind of grimaces and, 'Yeah, yeah,' from Democrats who said they thought their Republican colleagues would never work with them on criminal-justice reform or that our coalition might be interested only in white-collar issues."

In these sessions, Walsh sought to highlight stories that would resonate with conservatives while showing potential allies on the left the Heritage-NACDL coalition was serious about abuses of street-level defendants. He found this sweet spot in a series of ludicrous prosecutions that saw ex-offenders sent back to prison for many years because they accidentally came into contact with guns or bullets, technically violating the prohibition on felons possessing firearms. The breakthrough for over-criminalization came in 2009, when Heritage and NACDL began sharing the results of a joint study showing how Congress was eroding the "guilty mind" requirement. With this ammunition, Heritage and NACDL persuaded Democratic Rep. Bobby Scott of Virginia and Republican Rep. Louie Gohmert of Texas to cosponsor hearings on the issue. Walsh recalled that Gohmert, a former judge who had served in the army as a defense attorney, was convinced the Heritage effort was intellectually sound and rooted in conservative principles after a personal conversation with Meese, whom he admired.[37]

The Gohmert-Scott hearings featured testimony from victims of dubious white-collar prosecutions, but several speakers connected that problem to the overly harsh enforcement of street crime. One witness, a former member of the U.S. Sentencing Commission, argued that drug-related mandatory-minimum sentences had forced the commission to skew penalties upward across the board, including for white-collar crimes.[38] In his opening statement at the second hearing, Scott declared, "We can see the impact of the unfair and vague legislation at the hands of overzealous prosecutors when we look at the prison population. We now have on a daily basis over 2.3 million people locked up in our nation's prisons." Gohmert responded that he differed with Scott on sentencing for "true crimes," which he defined as violent, but otherwise did not push back. This was a signal that the causes of rolling back "over-criminalization" and the fight against "mass incarceration" were increasingly being viewed as compatible, if not essentially joined.[39]

As the loose network running from Prison Fellowship to the Heritage Foundation registered more and more legislative success, and as its members grew increasingly committed, it created a sense within the conservative movement that the crime issue was no longer owned by law-and-order traditionalists. Instead, it had become a signature cause of evangelicals, civil libertarians, and fiscal conservatives who defined the chief problem as inhumane government overreach that threatened rather than advanced public safety. This momentum, in turn, encouraged other ambitious conservatives to reexamine the criminal-justice issue on both ideological and political grounds.

MOMENTUM FOR CHANGE

Reformers caught another strong tailwind in 2010. The Tea Party wave of the midterm elections swept into office a new generation of conservatives eager to buck "establishment" positions with views they could argue were new, more authentically conservative. Two of these legislators, Utah Senator Mike Lee and Kentucky Senator Rand Paul, swiftly made the connection between Tea Party anti-statism and mass incarceration, introducing separate proposals to scale back or eliminate mandatory-minimum sentencing. Lawmakers on the right of the House GOP caucus have also taken up the cause. For example, Tea Party lawmakers Raul Labrador and Tom Massie pushed companions to the Lee and Paul bills, respectively.[40] In 2009, Ted Poe of Texas, a former judge, cosponsored his own mandatory-minimum reform, inspired by the case of two Border Patrol agents who drew stiff minimum sentences for wrongfully shooting a suspect.[41] Utah's Jason Chaffetz has pushed legislation allowing federal prisoners to earn time off their sentences if they worked on self-improvement (an effort later joined by Tea Party champion Trey Gowdy). Chaffetz would also go on to cofound a bipartisan caucus on justice reform.[42]

The year 2010 also became a landmark one because Congress finally managed to reduce the disparity in penalties for crack and powder-cocaine offenses—the issue Nolan had unsuccessfully worked on from prison 15 years earlier. The measure was cosponsored in the Senate by Sessions, who had championed the cause since 2001.[43] Sessions had also sponsored the Prison Rape Elimination Act, but neither position was suggestive of a broader evolution. A former U.S. Attorney and Alabama Attorney General, Sessions has maintained his support for tough sentencing overall while embracing efforts to roll back gross injustices—a model that implies such extreme cases are outliers, not signifiers of a systemic problem. (Tellingly, his initial cocaine bill would have narrowed the gap between crack and powder in part by increasing sentences for the latter.) Nonetheless, both the PREA and crack episodes created an opportunity for conservatives with a broader agenda to build their profile and cast the problems as symptomatic rather than exceptional. Prison Fellowship played an important deputy role on the crack issue, consulting with Sessions's office, submitting hearing testimony or recruiting other speakers, and collecting endorsements.[44] Easing crack penalties was a bolder leap than many religious conservatives were willing to publicly support, but it was remarkable that Nolan still got two faith groups, the National Association of Evangelicals and CitizenLink, the political arm of Focus on the Family, to endorse the change.[45] Meanwhile, Keene, Norquist, Nolan, and Hutchinson (the former Drug Enforcement Agency director) all signed a letter to House Speaker John Boehner backing the reform.[46] The final bill reduced the disparity to 18-1.

The bigger question was whether Congress would prove willing to go beyond the Sessions approach and tackle justice reform writ large. That was Jim Webb's vision. The centrist Virginia Democrat in 2009 began pushing a plan for a "National Criminal Justice Commission" to review the justice system top-to-bottom, at both federal and state levels. He failed, for reasons both institutional and partisan. As an outsider to the Judiciary Committee, he was treading on other senators' turf in an institution where prerogatives are jealously guarded. It is also true, however, that such a proposal coming from a Democrat, even a maverick like Webb, simply had lower chances of success than if it originated with the GOP. As FAMM's Julie Stewart wryly observed: "I was sorry he wasn't a Republican."[47] The initiative did get momentum, passing the House on a voice vote with no objections and also picking up bipartisan support in the Senate Judiciary Committee. Even so, 36 of the 39 Senate cosponsors were Democrats.[48] The Webb commission ultimately failed to overcome a filibuster by Republicans, who derided it as impinging on states' rights and biased toward Democratic control. Pressure to line up along partisan lines apparently grew at the 11th hour, with Senator John McCain surprising Webb by voting against the measure.[49] The issue did not come up again for a vote, and Webb left the Senate in 2013.

Just as Webb headed for the exits, however, two similar commission proposals originating with the GOP became reality.[50] The first was a proposal by Frank Wolf to establish a panel honoring Chuck Colson, who died in 2012. The warrant of the "Charles Colson Task Force on Federal

Corrections" was limited to the national system, but Wolf said he hoped that its recommendations would serve as a model for the states. Meanwhile, the over-criminalization hearings that Louie Gohmert held with Bobby Scott in 2010 were bearing fruit, as the House Judiciary Committee approved a special task force on the subject. Leadership of that panel was assigned to Scott and Jim Sensenbrenner, the Wisconsin Republican. In theory, the Colson commission had the broader mandate, but the over-criminalization task force aimed high and moved faster.

Scott and Sensenbrenner held hearings in 2013 and 2014, and the conversation quickly moved beyond the white-collar realm.[51] "Since we were working in a collegial manner, and you had many requests for a hearing on mandatory minimums specifically, and sentencing generally . . . it was natural that that would become one of the topics," Scott said. He added that the task force was able to operate carefully and take time to study the evidence. "With the over-criminalization task force, we had a deliberative process. We had a blank slate . . . Listen, there are a lot of initiatives that we know from research reduce crime and save money."[52] One of the initiatives highlighted at the hearings was the Texas experience. Right on Crime's Marc Levin testified about the state's 2007 reform and suggested they could be an example for the federal government.[53] Scott and Sensenbrenner took the message to heart: in early 2015, they asked Pew to help them develop a reform package modeled on its work in the states.[54]

For Sensenbrenner, the project marked a significant break with his previously orthodox tough-on-crime past. In 1993, the Wisconsin congressman had said he could not imagine reducing mandatory-minimum sentences for drug dealing or possession because drugs ripped at "the very fabric of our society."[55] In 1995, Sensenbrenner spoke out for giving states block grants to fight crime as they chose; he also voted to boost prison-construction funds over what the Clinton bill had authorized.[56] In the mid-2000s, Sensenbrenner served as chair of the House Judiciary Committee. From that perch, he led efforts to spotlight judges who frequently imposed sentences below the federal guidelines.[57] He also stirred up controversy by directly intervening in the case of a drug dealer whose eight-year sentence he considered too mild.[58]

But Sensenbrenner had also shown another side during his tenure at the Judiciary helm. He was instrumental in fighting off a series of amendments to the Second Chance Act that would have upset a delicate left-right compromise on the inclusion of faith-based organizations in the law.[59] The new, more deliberative climate on criminal justice that the Second Chance Act had established on the Hill also allowed Sensenbrenner to undergo a genuine learning experience. In June 2015, he told the *New York Times*, "We really aren't exposed to the practical aspect of the criminal-justice system, or what happens or doesn't happen in the prisons," adding that his investigation of the issues with Scott had been an "education."[60] The reform precedent from conservative states appears to have been an important component of that education. At the American Enterprise Institute in September, Sensenbrenner declared, "There is a better way. In recent years 27 states, particularly conservative, deeply red states, have enacted substantial reforms to their criminal-justice systems ... Many of the states have also seen a corresponding drop in crime. Their experience proves that we can reform the criminal-justice system without compromising public safety."[61]

While Scott and Sensenbrenner were poring over the data, a new factor came into play: the conservative turn on criminal justice began to register with the media, and with national liberals. In a city where polarization and grid-lock have become the dominant themes, the possibility of alliance between the likes of Rand Paul and New Jersey Democratic Senator Cory Booker became an irresistible "man-bites-dog" story—and an effective way for advocates to market their cause. In the spring of 2015, Newt Gingrich presided over a massive summit on criminal-justice reform together with Van Jones, a prominent liberal activist and Gingrich's cohost on the CNN show *Crossfire*.[62] Soon after, the Koch Brothers teamed up with the Arnold, Ford, and MacArthur Foundations to finance a new reform organization, the Coalition for Public Safety, with members spanning the political spectrum.[63]

These celebrations of bipartisanship have added brute political pressure to the processes of ideological conversion that drove earlier federal reforms. Senate Judiciary Committee Chairman Chuck Grassley, for example, remains severely critical of sentencing reform. Throughout 2014, Grassley remained adamantly opposed to adjusting mandatory minimums, even though he allowed his committee to vote on Mike Lee's reform bill. By 2015, the Iowan had moderated his stance and indicated a willingness to negotiate. In the fall, a bipartisan group of senators submitted a bill with Grassley's support, albeit with very narrow reforms.[64]

Republicans have also reveled in another "man-bites-dog" story related to criminal justice—the notion that this might be an issue on which they can effectively reach out to African Americans. As we argued in chapter 2, while conservative position-taking on law and order responded to a widely recognized problem, it also provided an opportunity for Republicans to respond to racial anxieties. President George W. Bush attempted to pivot away from a strategy of racial polarization as president with his vision of compassionate conservatism, an effort that Tea Party activists treated as symptomatic of all the problems of the Republican Party—too compromising and insufficiently anti-statist.

It did not take Republicans long to realize that, while they could turn their backs on compassionate conservatism, they still needed an appeal to African Americans, if only for the consumption of more moderate white voters.[65] In a party deeply shaped by the presence of the Tea Party, however, that appeal had to be consistent with anti-statism, rather than offering than a smaller version of the expanded state that Democrats had on offer. Crime turns out to be one of the few areas where that trick can be effectively pulled off. No one has made the argument that Republicans need to prioritize the cause of criminal justice as sharply as Rand Paul, who emerged as an outspoken, almost radical critic of mass incarceration. He has pilloried the drug war and the widespread disenfranchisement of felons and echoed the liberal critique of criminal justice as "The New Jim Crow." Paul has been unusually willing to discuss the issue in frankly racialized terms, observing in a speech at the historically black Bowie State University that "I tell people that I think they're not looking if they don't think that the incarceration problem in our country is not skewed towards one race. I don't think it's purposeful but I do think it is actual and it is real and we should do something about it."[66] Paul's willingness to address the racial component of criminal justice has been echoed by former governor Rick Perry. During his 2015 presidential bid, Perry began a major speech on equality of opportunity with a chilling description of a Texas lynching, before discussing, among other things, the need to reduce the scope of incarceration.[67]

Other prominent Republicans have put criminal justice reform squarely within the framework of developing a substantive agenda of equal opportunity for the disadvantaged. Paul Ryan, while head of the House Budget Committee, published a major report on "Expanding Opportunity in America," in which criminal justice was one of five areas that were highlighted as having a high payoff for increasing social mobility. Ryan's staff worked closely on that section with Robert Woodson of the Center for Neighborhood Enterprise, who is a longtime advocate for Republicans engaging more deeply with the interests of black America. Ryan's report spent considerable time lavishing praise on Texas and Georgia and using their reforms as a model for the federal government. The report, along with the work of other Republicans, suggests that Republican engagement with criminal justice is likely to have legs, because it responds to a recurrent problem of Republican political outreach while not crossing any Tea Party red lines—so far. As we will explain in the conclusion, rolling back prison populations will require some degree of alternative state-building, and the danger remains that this is a step further than conservatives will be willing to go.

The policy contagion that began in red states such as Georgia and Texas has now decisively spread to Washington, D.C. By the end of 2015, however, this changed tone had altered the policy conversation more than actual legislative outcomes. More ominously, there were signs that not all national Republicans were willing to retire the crime war's cudgels. Locked in a brutal presidential primary, Texas Senator Ted Cruz denounced Democrats as the party of violent criminals and voted against moving the Grassley compromise out of committee—even though he previously had co-sponsored a more sweeping reform bill himself. Arkansas Republican Senator Tom Cotton followed Cruz in attacking the Grassley bill, modest as it was.[68] So while the old tough-on-crime orthodoxy is on the defensive in American conservatism, it is far from dead. We turn next to the reform movement's prospects to consolidate its gains and strike lasting blows against mass incarceration.

CHAPTER 10

Mass Decarceration?

Twenty years ago, no one would have predicted that conservatives would move so far in rethinking their tough-on-crime position. Without this shift, the significant reforms in some of the nation's reddest states would have been impossible, and there would be much less room for progress at the federal level, or even in blue states. The conservative evolution has enabled the United States to finally break the persistent upward trajectory of incarceration and put in play the prospect of seriously reducing the nation's bloated prison population. It is entirely possible that this opportunity could be squandered, and in this chapter we consider the possibilities and perils ahead. First, however, we draw some lessons from what has been achieved: lessons that illuminate the possibilities for cross-partisan breakthroughs in our polarized age.

As important as the actions of individuals have been, it was shifts in larger structural conditions that largely undermined tough-on-crime's political potency. Unlike abortion, taxes, or climate change, Republican positions on criminal justice were not anchored by a powerful party coalition member. The glue holding those positions in place was not coalitional, but electoral and ideological: conservatives were punitive because it worked politically and because they believed that it was consistent with movement principles. As crime declined, the issue lost salience among the public and ceased to be a cornerstone of Republican electoral strategy. Meanwhile, activists were refashioning the Republican Party into a more consistently anti-statist mold, opening a window for conservatives to apply their long-standing skepticism of government to the correctional system. For conservatives at the state level, aggressive budget cutting made it increasingly difficult to keep giving corrections a pass.

The confluence of all these factors meant that conservative politicians, who just a few years before resisted criticism of mass incarceration as the bleating of out-of-touch liberals, became open to evidence that they once ignored, such as extraordinary rates of recidivism. Those seeking to replicate the success of conservative criminal justice reformers need to be cognizant, therefore, that while they started working in a hostile climate, by the time of their greatest breakthroughs the political weather had shifted considerably. They were working with the grain of structural political forces, not against them.

Each of the structural preconditions that enabled the conservative evolution on criminal justice suggests a criterion for determining which policies are promising for developing trans-partisan coalitions, and which are not. First, change is unlikely if a position is anchored by a major coalition partner, which criminal justice was not. Our parties are like strong alliances between nation-states, in which there is a system of collective security—an attack on one is an attack on all. To champion or even to accede to a change in policy hostile to the perceived interest of a major coalition member is an invitation to that member to bolt the party, a weighty choice that will not be made without the most significant potential gains. Second, change is only possible if an issue is not working electorally, since even the shrewdest advocacy cannot convince a working politician to give up a weapon in a competitive election. Third, changes in conservative positions are, almost exclusively, likely to happen on issues that involve encouraging them to be even more resolutely anti-statist. Cutting the Pentagon budget,[1] encouraging a less ambitious foreign policy, reining in surveillance, and restraining occupational licensing or agricultural subsidies all fit that framework. By contrast, there is little reason to expect trans-partisanship to spread to expansions of the welfare state, environmental regulation, or the level of taxation.[2]

Our story shows that even when the structural criteria for a position change are met, change is far from automatic. In fact, much of the initial work of changing minds and forming low-profile coalitions of elite actors began before it was clear that the macro-politics of the issue changed. If Chuck Colson, Pat Nolan, or Julie Stewart had waited until those conditions had shifted, the infrastructure that eventually discovered and exploited that opportunity would not have been in place. The result would have been a far more muted response, or even an entirely missed opportunity.

It takes an unusual sort of political advocate to fight against the consensus of their own party, with little hope for change. They will typically be people fired by a particularly intense moral conviction, and often by a searing personal experience. Conservatives shifted position on criminal justice because, at least initially, a small number of such leaders decided that the party's position was problematic, and were willing to use their personal credibility to persuade influential elites to rethink their position. These leaders were perfectly happy to use pragmatic considerations like the impact of incarceration on state budgets to persuade legislators, but they were all driven to engage with the issue by much deeper personal, ideological, or even spiritual motivations.

These internal dissenters had important external allies, but their powerful personal stories and scars from previous ideological battles made it nearly impossible to attack them as tools of those outside the movement. Their reputations allowed them to make a rhetorical move that is especially significant in a polarized political environment: to claim that a switch in position meant becoming *more* authentically conservative. Until recently they mostly avoided high-profile hand-holding across ideological lines (even though there was a great deal of cooperation behind the scenes), in order to preserve the (basically accurate) impression that this was an authentically conservative movement.

Just as it is true that advocates and funders cannot hope for change in party positions on any issue they choose, it is also the case that they cannot produce effective advocates for such change out of thin air. Those who can persuasively make the case to ideological true believers are not the moderates whom those on the other side might prefer to work with, but those who have ideological credibility and a story to tell about why, despite being every bit as strident as those whose minds they seek to change, they saw the way to a new position. Jay Neal and Pat Nolan and Julie Stewart had such stories. Much of the critical work in this process happens well before an issue has become safe for popular consumption, which suggests that funders need to be willing to commit when conditions seem darkest, and when it is unclear whether change will ever happen. And then they need to be willing to hold on for as long as it takes.[3]

All that said, conservatives did not bravely make this change by themselves, with nary a nonconservative to be found. While the original funding for TPPF's work on criminal justice came from the rock-ribbed Tim Dunn, most of the money since has come from the centrist Pew Foundation, and some from the very left-of-center Public Welfare Foundation. In most states the serious work of actually putting together legislative options and hashing out tough compromises was done by Pew and the Council of State Governments and, in some places, the ACLU. It is a measure of the effectiveness of their work that all of these center and left advocates managed to support conservatives while not doing anything to compromise their credibility. It is a mark of their talent and restraint in seeking credit that there have been no major counterattacks presenting conservative reformers as mere puppets for liberal funders, which is precisely what happened to evangelicals who supported measures to address global warming.[4] These outsiders let conservatives make arguments that they were not always happy with, knowing that their right-wing allies needed to speak in a language that was internally authentic.

HOW REFORM COULD GO WRONG

Conservatives have embraced reforms that they would have treated as anathema only a few years ago. Despite this momentum, the potential for conservatives to support even more ambitious reform could be squandered and the progress made to date could be reversed. In this section, we will discuss the reasons for pessimism, while in the next we will present the—on balance more persuasive—reasons for optimism.

The greatest threat to criminal justice reform is not that it blows up in a wave of backlash, but that it fizzles out. One of the main tropes of conservative reformers is that, while the tough measures of the '80s and '90s were necessary, they went overboard in including too many stiff sentences for nonviolent offenders. Newt Gingrich's comments, at a major event sponsored by the Pew Charitable Trusts, are characteristic of this argument: "There are several thousand people alive today who would not have been if we had continued the patterns of the early '90s. In that sense being tough on crime is legitimate. And when you talk about violent crime I'm prepared to defend a very tough sentence and a very tough approach to people who either rape or kill other people. But the fact was there were tremendous unintended consequences. The truth is, locking up people who were engaged in very minor drug offenses destroyed their future, it didn't teach them a lesson and it didn't seem to have an effect on convincing the rest of the community."[5]

A sharp division between violent and nonviolent offenders is consistent with the Pew-style reforms that conservatives have signed on to in state after state. But it is unlikely to get the cause of reducing mass incarceration much further, for the simple reason that the majority of people (54 percent) in state prison are there for violent crimes. Another 19 percent are behind bars for property crimes. Just 16 percent are in for drug crimes, and a mere 3.7 percent for simple drug possession.[6] To cut the prison population by half within the widely accepted framework that Gingrich articulates, everyone but violent criminals—chronic drunk drivers, burglars, peddlers of illegal guns—would stay on the street. This is, to say the least, highly unlikely. The hard reality is that the bulk of the prison population is there for offenses that most people think deserve some prison time. And even if we agreed to give all nonviolent criminals probation, even within the most effective programs many would inevitably flunk out, with prison the only remaining option. In short, cutting prison populations substantially will require that we rethink the length of sentences for serious crimes, and eliminate prison time entirely for a significant chunk of others.

Another reason for concern is an increase in the salience of crime. It was the enormous drop in offending, and the related drop in public fear, that provided a window for conservatives to become more open to information on the damage caused by mass incarceration, and more sympathetic to criminals and their families. The spike in homicides in major cities during 2015 showed how easily crime can come thundering back into the headlines. Done right, criminal-justice reform should contribute rather than detract from efforts to bring these localized homicide crises under control. But when public fear rises, it becomes harder for politicians to let go of their tried-and-true formulas of more severity.

The danger is exacerbated by the polarizing context in which the homicides have been covered—the firestorm of protest over police brutality against African Americans. The controversies in Ferguson, Baltimore, Chicago, New York, and other cities threaten to wrap the crime issue in an older, politicized dichotomy between accused rioters and criminals (generally defended by liberals) and cops (defended by conservatives). There is a serious risk that conservatives will turn away from their recent anti-statism—and its skepticism of law enforcement—and back toward their older emphasis on social order.

Still, it is unlikely the clock can be turned back completely on conservative reform. Consider Chris Christie. The New Jersey governor and former GOP presidential candidate has asserted that police are under assault by liberals. But even in the same breath, Christie has taken credit for reductions in his state's prison population. Shortly before President Obama was scheduled to visit New Jersey to talk about criminal justice, Christie argued that President Obama "does not support law enforcement," and added: "He's going to come today to New Jersey to a place, where under my tenure, we have reduced crime by 20 percent and reduced the prison population by 10 percent ... He has absolutely nothing to do with it."

More broadly, the conservative evolution on criminal justice has coincided with the growth of a more assertive liberal critique of mass incarceration's roots in racial injustice. So far, these two tracks have not collided, and as noted in chapter 9, conservatives with a national profile have come quite far in acknowledging the racial dimensions of the prison problem. Conservatives' analysis of how that problem came about will rarely if ever match that of the left. Sen. Mike Lee, for example, argues that, "For conservatives, the process of reform begins by recognizing not the mistakes of our past, but the successes, because the dysfunction that we see in today's status quo is more often the product of good intentions gone awry and sound policies grown old than the manifestation of historical or structural inequities." Comments like this are almost perfectly calibrated to deny critics of mass incarceration on the left a full accounting of conservatives' responsibility for the mess we are in. This is a pill liberals will have to swallow if we are to see further progress. Both at the federal level and in Southern states with strong conservative majorities—states where really dramatic change must happen if national rates of imprisonment are to drop to where they need to go— advocates need to accept that change will come through further shifts on the right, or not at all.

Reform can also get waylaid by good old-fashioned petty politics. While Oklahoma went through a JRI process in 2012, few of the changes were effectively implemented, and the state has seen one of the highest increases in incarceration in the nation over the past few years. In its political culture, partisan balance and historical commitment to high levels of incarceration, Oklahoma is a close match with Texas, which is the poster boy for conservative reform. And while they came five years later, the reforms in Oklahoma closely tracked those originally passed in Texas. But as soon as they were passed, Gov. Mary Fallin pulled back her commitment to funding the program and creating the oversight committees necessary to put it into place. The program became trapped in conflict between the state legislature and the governor's office over political credit and control, with some of the governor's advisors whispering in her ear that the legislation was suspiciously "liberal." In particular, it appears that Fallin was concerned that the initiative was too tied to Speaker of the House Kris Steele, and that it required that she give up too much direct executive control.[7]

Yet another reason for concern is that the greatest strides made by conservatives so far have been in bright red states, such as Texas, Georgia, and Mississippi, where Republicans have little effective political competition, and thus no fear of giving up on an issue that might provide ammunition with which to snipe at Democrats. Republicans in purple states, facing very different political calculations, may not be willing to move as far. For instance, in Virginia, which has largely taken a pass on the reforms made by other states, Democratic Governor Terry McCauliffe has called for a commission to study the changes that have passed by huge majorities in more conservative states (including bringing back parole, which the state abolished two decades ago).

The response of Republicans in the state legislature could have been taken directly from newspapers 25 years ago. For example, C. Todd Gilbert, a former prosecutor who represents Shenandoah, declared: "I'm sure he's getting a tremendous amount of pressure from the base of his party to tear down the criminal justice system. Criminal apologists would love nothing more than to have no one serve any time for practically anything."[8] That is not the kind of rhetoric that is conducive to the reforms that Republicans in other states have enthusiastically supported.

In Michigan, Republicans responded to a justice-reform initiative by former Democratic Gov. Jennifer Granholm with similar hostility. Republicans in bright blue California have responded to the restructuring of their state's criminal-justice system, pushed through by Democrats to comply with a massive federal lawsuit over prison conditions, with similar saber-rattling.[9] In purple states where they are worried about giving up a political weapon, and in blue states where they are cut out of the legislative process entirely, Republicans have much less of an incentive to change than their red state brethren.

Perhaps the least discussed reason for concern, and the one with the most potential to throw sand in the gears of reform, is that while conservatives have effectively helped put reform on the agenda, the alternatives that they are pushing could be ineffective or even perverse. Many conservative states have put additional resources, and a great deal of hope, into drug courts and in-prison addiction treatment. Both are helpful when carefully targeted on the hardest cases, but are too expensive and insufficiently scalable to provide to all drug-involved offenders, and are a waste of resources for the majority who are capable of functioning with a lower level of support.[10]

Meanwhile, most conservative reform states have expanded the use of parole and probation. But without major improvements in the quality and professionalism of these systems—which while they are cheaper than prison, cost real money and require a commitment to the quality of public service—they are unlikely to effectively prevent ex-offenders from heading back to prison. As Robert Weisberg and Joan Petersilia have argued, this could lead to a new wave of public safety pessimism, in which older concerns that "nothing works" would return.[11] The window for building the bureaucratic culture of well-managed, sustainable alternatives to incarceration may not be open long, and without it politicians (especially in conservative states) are unlikely to be enthusiastic about draining the prison population. Building high-status administrative cultures and drawing talented people into public service has not been a feature of the politics of our most conservative states in the last few years, and without doing so there are severe limits on how deeply prisons can be drained and offenders effectively supervised in the community. Alliances with interest groups could make the problem worse: Already, private prison operators and bail bondsmen are jumping at the opportunity to get into the parole and probation business. In fact, representatives of the bail bond industry already sit in meetings of ALEC's public safety task force, and have had a major legislative impact on otherwise reform-minded Mississippi.[12]

Conservative and liberal advocates have so far cooperated mainly behind the scenes, which allowed Republicans to take ownership over the issue and claim that their shift was ideologically pure. Increasingly, however, liberals and conservatives have taken to sitting together on a podium singing from the same hymnal. The Coalition for Public

Safety has brought together groups on the right, such as Right on Crime, Freedom Works, and Americans for Tax Reform, with the left-leaning ACLU and Center for American Progress, all funded by donors on the right such as Koch Industries and the left like the MacArthur Foundation.

This cooperation has certainly generated headlines and a perception that this is an issue whose "time has come." However, in a highly polarized environment, the close cooperation between conservatives and liberals could diminish the very valuable perception among legislators on the right that reform is something that they are doing for their own fiscal or religious reasons. Those same legislators may not have the same enthusiasm for a bipartisan, increasingly centrist project whose advocates are seen as too eager to join hands with those on the left. This may be an increasing risk as reforms get tougher and the need for effective identity vouching becomes even greater.

CAUSES FOR HOPE

There are more than enough reasons for long-term pessimism about conservatives' commitment to reform, reasons that advocates and funders would ignore at their peril. On balance, however, we believe the forces on the side of optimism are more compelling. Those forces only determine the *odds* of success or failure, however. How criminal justice policy will look a decade hence will be determined by the skill with which advocates play the hands they have been given, as well as a good dose of luck.

As we argued in chapter 2, the growth of the carceral state was driven by some very powerful path-dependent processes. Expansions of mass incarceration did not produce pendulum-like countereffects, but generated reinforcing feedback that encouraged policymakers to push even further in the direction of punitive policymaking. Could it be that the change in conservative policy preferences has helped turn this policymaking machine in reverse? Are there signs that reinforcing feedback is now operating in a way that turns even rather small decarcerating reforms into a springboard for more ambitious action? If so, what are the mechanisms generating a virtuous cycle of anti-carceral state reforms?

In the punitive era policymakers were encouraged to continue piling up longer sentences because they learned that it paid serious political returns. Like the mouse who gets rewarded with a piece of cheese each time he presses on the right lever, policymakers who pulled the incarceration lever continually received pleasing benefits from voters and supportive interest groups. So they kept pulling, ignoring the negative consequences of doing so.

The benefits of continually pulling the punitive lever have drastically diminished in an era in which voters' anxieties around crime are much less acute, while there are increasing rewards to those who support measures that reduce severity. Republican governors like Rick Perry and Nathan Deal have found that supporting reform brings them national attention, while allowing them to speak to constituencies, especially African Americans, to whom they would otherwise have nothing to say. The Republican political consulting class has gotten the message, with younger analysts like Kristen Soltis Anderson recommending that Republicans embrace criminal-justice reform as a way to reach Millennial voters.[13] If conservative politicians come to believe that taking on reform is actually politically valuable (and not merely neutral), that would give the cause much more urgency than it has had up until now.

Even modest reforms appear to whet the appetite of conservative policymakers for more. The experience of Georgia suggests that initial reforms are the equivalent of dipping legislators' toes in the water. Once they realize that the water is warm, in the sense that there are no obvious negative political consequences, they are receptive when their leaders ask them to do more. The examples of Texas and Georgia also show that, as they make successive votes, conservatives are also building up more knowledge about alternatives to incarceration and the costs of prisons, which increase their appetite to do more and their confidence that this new policy direction will actually work.

Back in 2007, conservatives in Texas started off the wave of conservative criminal justice reform without any compelling red-state models to emulate. That has changed enormously in the years since. With each reform passed in a sister red state, it is easier for conservatives to justify more ambitious action at home. In fact, in a pattern that resembles the welfare reforms of the 1980s and 1990s,[14] conservatives are increasingly eager to compete for leadership in the cause of reform, which should push them to go bigger and bolder. In addition, conservatives are being fed new ideas for reform through increasingly dense inter-state policymaking networks. Every year ALEC passes along new model legislation that reaches into new areas of the criminal justice system, and SPN and Right on Crime publicize reforms made in other states. The further one reform package goes, therefore, the greater incentive there is to go even further with the next, and the larger the menu of existing, vetted reforms from which conservative policymakers have to draw on.

In the 1980s and 1990s, national politicians set a martial tone, with their doomsday rhetoric about drugs and the infamous Willie Horton commercial, that encouraged states to double down on incarceration. In policy terms, too, the feds promoted building prison beds over experimenting with alternatives. As the federal government got tougher on drug crimes and enacted mandatory minimum sentences, it provided a model for states that had not already done so to move in the same direction. The 1994 crime bill even dangled prison-building funds before states that agreed to reduce their use of parole.

The federal government is no longer prodding the states toward greater severity, and slowly—more slowly than many states—is joining the cause of rethinking mass incarceration. Just as the federal government picked up innovations in severity from states in the 1980s and 1990s and encouraged the remaining states to follow along, it may be that the more ambitious reform states are providing a template today for the federal government, which will help spread the cause to the currently recalcitrant. The next step would be for the federal government to actively provide resources for reform, as it did in a more modest way in funding JRI efforts, including competitions like "Race to the Top" to push states to go to the limit of their comfort zone in reform. Finally, the federal government could provide substantial resources for policy evaluation and research, to ensure that reform effort is focused on those changes with the greatest potential to reduce incarceration while protecting public safety.

There is wide agreement that, among the forces that pushed prison numbers skyward, few were as important as prosecutors. Not only did district attorneys crack down on the offenders police brought their way, but they indicted more and dismissed fewer than they had before. In many states, prosecutors played a direct role in pushing legislators to give them more "tools" in the form of new offenses and punishments, a role supported by the fact that so many legislators came from a background as prosecutors. In the tough-on-crime era, few politicians dared to cross prosecutors. In fact, just a few years ago in Indiana, Gov. Mitch Daniels took on the reform cause but, unlike Nathan Deal in Georgia, failed to find legislative champions willing to fight back against the opposition of prosecutors.[15]

While prosecutors are still a fearsome player in the politics of criminal justice, they are increasingly isolated. In Georgia, for example, prosecutors got the message that senior Republican leaders were solidly behind a new policy direction and chose to avoid the strategy of maximum confrontation. As policy shifts against prosecutors (and other law-enforcement interests) in those states where they previously had a legislative stranglehold, the incentives for prosecutors to stand in the way will continually diminish. As marginal policymakers see prosecutors pulling in their fangs, they may be willing to be more ambitious than they otherwise might have been. And as policymakers push harder, the incentives for prosecutors to shift even further will increase—a textbook model of reinforcing feedback.

Meanwhile, there seems to be a genuine change of heart occurring among segments of the prosecutorial community. Dozens of former high-ranking federal prosecutors have endorsed reform of federal sentencing. Progressive district attorneys have been elected in Milwaukee, Houston, and San Francisco. With the reformist brand now in vogue, and with the media increasingly enamored of the storyline that criminal justice is broken, such outliers are likely to accrue substantial prestige beyond their profession. If carrots do not work, the fact that reformers are openly talking about targeting especially aggressive prosecutors electorally might get their attention. If enough resources are put into prosecutorial elections, it could reverse the perception that no one ever lost their DA job by being too harsh.

In the previous section we observed that one of the most significant risks to the momentum of conservative reform is the "violent/non-violent offender trap." That is a real risk. It will be significantly attenuated, however, by the hard-wiring of the language and analytical tools of "evidence-based practices" and "performance measurement" into how conservatives think about criminal justice. Conservatives have already accepted that, for non-violent offenders, the primary consideration should be forward-looking (the likelihood of future offending) rather than backward looking (punishment). While the instinct to punish will never wholly disappear (nor should it), the spread of risk assessment should make the costs of very long sentences a much more salient part of decisions about what to do with resources in the future. A substantial body of research, for example, shows that most offenders "age out" of crime around age 40, and there is very little crime reduction value to keeping them behind bars for decades after that age.[16] Moreover, bundling all "violent offenders" together under one rubric makes little sense. A robber is not a murderer. A crime of passion is not cold-blooded predation.

There is some evidence that conservatives appreciate these points. Gingrich himself told a reporter, offstage, after his public remarks at the Pew event: "There are people who do things that are clearly not violent but who are techni-cally labeled as violent—so you have to ask yourself, what's the purpose of that? When I worry about violent crime, I worry about someone who has the potential to harm you or me. And those people, I think, should be kept off the street until they're too old to threaten anybody. And I'm prepared to be very tough with genuinely violent criminals. But I don't want to have a broad, sweeping series of laws that become felonies that in fact shouldn't be felonies."[17] And as we saw in chapter 8, Nathan Deal has deployed the violent/non-violent distinction to raise similar questions about who is cast as violent.

Until then, there is still plenty of low-hanging fruit. For examples, conservatives are only beginning to turn their attention to jails, which are stuffed full of people in pre-trial detention, in de-facto mental hospitalization, and in petty sentences on misdemeanor charges. The conservative reform spirit hasn't reached localities as much as states, and thus the cold eye of cost-benefit analysis hasn't exposed their high cost and limited (or perverse) crime-control effects. If the conservative criminal justice infrastructure grows deep enough to work in a serious way below the state level, it is easy to imagine draining the jail population as well as those in prison.

While left-of-center donors have been committed to the cause of criminal justice for decades, until recently conservative organizations had few funders on their own side of the fence willing to support the cause. Many conservative state think tanks, for example, have been interested in engaging more deeply on the issue but have failed to do so because of an absence of donor interest. The Philanthropy Roundtable, the main organization of conservative donors, has devoted panel after panel at its annual meetings to criminal justice, but failed to lure many of its members.

That appears to be changing. In particular, the entry of the Koch family into criminal justice could provide what has been lacking over the last decade, which is a wealthy donor willing to bankroll a deep bench able to keep the issue of reform on the agenda of state legislatures and ensure the durability of past reforms. While the experience of the Kochs as think tank patrons is not entirely reassuring, it could be quite positive if it signals to other donors that they should turn their attention to the nation's prisons and jails.[18]

With 2.3 million people under lock and key, bringing incarceration in America to a reasonable level will be a decades-long project. Such an effort can only be sustained if liberals and conservatives alike come to see it as an extension of their most fundamental values. We are still a long way from that level of commitment. There is reason for optimism, however, in how far conservatives have come from the days when they shut their eyes to the human and financial costs of incarceration. With every day that passes, their eyes open a little wider.

Notes

Preface

1. Newt Gingrich, "Toward a Drug Free America: A Proposal for an Effective War on Cocaine and Heroin," House Democratic Strategy for the Cocaine Issue in 1986, July 29, 1986, folder "Drug Initiative II," series "Office of the Chief of Staff," Box 12, W. Dennis Thomas files, Ronald Reagan Library.
2. Ibid.
3. Mike Christensen, "Florida, Not Mass., Gave Convict 'Early Release': [CITY Edition]," *St. Petersburg Times*, September 21, 1988, sec. National.
4. Mike Christensen, "Comparing Democrats to Noriega, Gingrich Urges GOP War on Crime," *The Atlanta Journal and the Atlanta Constitution*, May 19, 1989, sec. National News.
5. Grover G. Norquist, "Making Crime Pay," *The American Spectator*, May 1993.
6. Jim Abrams, "US Rate of Incarceration Is 2d Highest in World, Study Finds; Russia 1st: [City Edition]," *Boston Globe*, September 13, 1994, sec. National/Foreign; "U.S. Incarceration Rate Highest in the World: [Final Edition]," *The Ottawa Citizen*, January 5, 1991, sec. News.
7. "The Republican 'Contract with America,'" 1994, http://wps.prenhall.com/wps/media/objects/434/445252/DocumentsLibrary/docs/contract.htm.
8. Steven M. Gillon, "The Gingrich Revolution and the Roots of Republican Dysfunction," *The Huffington Post*, October 12,

2015, http://www.huffingtonpost.com/steven-m-gillon/the-gingrich-revolution-a_b_8272054.html.

9. "Reno Attacks GOP Prison Proposal," *UPI NewsTrack*, February 9, 1995; Catalina Camia, "GOP's Crime Bill Advances—Clinton Promise of Veto Repeated," *The Dallas Morning News*, February 15, 1995, Washington Bureau edition, sec. News; Holly Idelson, "House Committee Clears Prison-Funding Increase," *The Washington Times*, February 2, 1995, 2 edition, sec. A Nation 104th Congress: 100-Day Countdown.

10. *Last Sacred Cow Briefing: Grover Norquist, Americans for Tax Reform*, 2011, http://www.youtube.com/watch?v=HWuhGR0T R80&feature=youtube_gdata_player.

11. Newt Gingrich and Pat Nolan, "Prison Reform: A Smart Way for States to Save Money and Lives," *The Washington Post*, January 7, 2011, sec. Opinions, http://www.washingtonpost.com/wp-dyn/content/article/2011/01/06/AR2011010604386.html.

12. "Economic Opportunity for All Americans," *Perry for President*, accessed July 3, 2015, https://rickperry.org/economic-opportunity-for-all-americans.

13. "Debate Prep: What the GOP Presidential Candidates Are Saying About Criminal Justice Reform," *U.S. Justice Action Network*, 2015, http://www.justiceactionnetwork.org/debate-prep-what-the-gop-presidential-candidates-are-saying-about-criminal-justice-reform/.

14. Steven Teles, Heather Hurlburt, and Mark Schmitt, "Philanthropy in a Time of Polarization," *Stanford Social Innovation Review*, Summer 2014, http://ssir.org/articles/entry/philanthropy_in_a_time_of_polarization.ng.

Chapter 1

1. David Dagan and Steven M. Teles, "The Social Construction of Policy Feedback: Incarceration, Conservatism, and Ideological Change," *Studies in American Political Development* 29 (October 2015): 1–27.

2. This is a basic finding of self-categorization theory, which is summarized in Stephen Reicher, Russell Spears, and S. Alexander Haslam, "The Social Identity Approach in Social Psychology," in *The SAGE Handbook of Identities*, eds. Margaret

Wetherell and Chandra Talpade Mohanty (London: SAGE Publications, 2010), pgs. 45–62.

3. Geoffrey L. Cohen et al., "Bridging the Partisan Divide: Self-Affirmation Reduces Ideological Closed-Mindedness and Inflexibility in Negotiation," *Journal of Personality and Social Psychology* 93, no. 3 (September 2007): 415–30; Dan M. Kahan, "Ideology, Motivated Reasoning, and Cognitive Reflection," *Judgment and Decision Making* 8, no. 4 (2013): 407–24; Raymond S. Nickerson, "Confirmation Bias: A Ubiquitous Phenomenon in Many Guises," *Review of General Psychology* 2, no. 2 (June 1998): 187; Charles Taber and Milton Lodge, "Motivated Skepticism in the Evaluation of Political Beliefs," *American Journal of Political Science* 50, no. 3 (July 2006): 755–69.

4. Geoffrey L. Cohen, "Party over Policy: The Dominating Impact of Group Influence on Political Beliefs," *Journal of Personality and Social Psychology* 85, no. 5 (November 2003): 808–22; Dan Kahan et al., "Who Fears the HPV Vaccine, Who Doesn't, and Why? An Experimental Study of the Mechanisms of Cultural Cognition," *Law and Human Behavior* 34 (2010): 501–16; Donald Braman, Dan Kahan, and James Grimmelmann, "Modeling Facts, Culture, and Cognition in the Gun Debate," *Social Justice Research* 18, no. 3 (September 2005): 283–304.

5. Michael Tonry, "Evidence, Ideology, and Politics in the Making of American Criminal Justice Policy," *Crime and Justice* 42, no. 1 (August 1, 2013): 1–18, doi:10.1086/671382.

6. Kristen A. Hughes, "Justice Expenditure and Employment in the United States, 2003," Justice Expenditure and Employment Series (Bureau of Justice Statistics, April 1, 2006), http://www.bjs.gov/index.cfm?ty=pbdetail&iid=1017.

7. Jack Bascom Brooks, "Comprehensive Crime Control Act of 1990," Report on Public Bill, 14017 H.rp.681/1 (House Committee on the Judiciary, September 5, 1990), ; Stephen Wermiel, "U.S. Sentencing Proposals Spur Worries Over Inmate Rise, Cost of New Prisons," *Wall Street Journal, Eastern Edition*, June 22, 1987; White, "The Illogical Lockup: [3 Star Edition]," *Orlando Sentinel*, April 27, 1987, sec. Editorial Page; Dave McNeely, "Key Legislators Question Borrowing for Prison Construction: [Final Edition],"

Austin American Statesman, January 19, 1989, sec. City/State; David Poulson and Grand Rapids Press Bureau, "Officials, Taxpayers Struggle with Fiscal Drain of Prisons," *The Grand Rapids Press*, February 16, 1992; Stuart Taylor Jr., "Strict Penalties for Criminals: Pendulum of Feeling Swings," *New York Times, Late Edition (East Coast)*, December 13, 1983, sec. A; Michael C. Campbell and Heather Schoenfeld, "The Transformation of America's Penal Order: A Historicized Political Sociology of Punishment," *American Journal of Sociology* 118, no. 5 (March 2013): 1375–423; Adam Yeomans, "Senate Leader Backs Stop Bill," *Tallahassee Democrat*, January 11, 1995.

8. "Most Ex-Inmates Rearrested Within 3 Years, Study Finds," *The Washington Post*, April 3, 1989, Final edition, sec. A, Chicago Tribune wires, "Study: 62% of Freed Inmates Rearrested within 3 Years: [Final, M Edition]," *Chicago Tribune*.

9. Sharon LaFraniere, "Study Cites Benefits of Prison Job Training; Recidivism Lower in Inmates Who Worked," *The Washington Post*, January 2, 1992, Final edition, sec. a, ProQuest; "Tying State Funding to Recidivism Is Key," *Austin American Statesman*, September 7, 1995, sec. Editorials, ProQuest Central; Franklin E. Zimring, "The Truth About Sex Offenders; California: Wilson's Claim of 75% Recidivism Is Refuted by the State's Own Statistics; Most Convicts Don't 'Keep Doing It,'" *Los Angeles Times*, May 5, 1997, Home edition, sec. Metro; Part B.

10. For an argument that in-prison rehabilitative programs remained remarkably stable in both scope and content throughout the 1980s, see Michelle S. Phelps, "Rehabilitation in the Punitive Era: The Gap between Rhetoric and Reality in U.S. Prison Programs" (Author Manuscript, March 2011), http://www.ncbi.nlm.nih.gov/pmc/articles/PMC3762476/ #!po=96.1538.

11. Newt Gingrich and Pat Nolan, "Prison Reform: A Smart Way for States to Save Money and Lives," *The Washington Post*, January 7, 2011, sec. Opinions, http://www.washingtonpost. com/wp-dyn/content/article/2011/01/06/AR2011010604386. html; Vikrant P. Reddy and Marc A. Levin, "The Conservative

Case Against More Prisons," *The American Conservative*, March 6, 2013, http://www.theamericanconservative.com/articles/the-conservative-case-against-more-prisons/; Richard A. Viguerie, "A Conservative Case for Prison Reform," *The New York Times*, June 9, 2013, sec. Opinion, http://www.nytimes.com/2013/06/10/opinion/a-conservative-case-for-prison-reform.html; Ken Cuccinelli and Deborah Daniels, "Less Incarceration Could Lead to Less Crime," *The Washington Post*, June 19, 2014, http://www.washingtonpost.com/opinions/less-incarceration-could-lead-to-less-crime/2014/06/19/03f0e296-ef0e-11e3-bf76-447a5df6411f_story.html.

12. "State of Recidivism: The Revolving Door of America's Prisons" (Pew Center on the States, April 2011), http://www.pewtrusts.org/en/research-and-analysis/reports/0001/01/01/state-of-recidivism.

13. Khalil Gibran Muhammad, *The Condemnation of Blackness: Race, Crime, and the Making of Modern Urban America* (Cambridge, MA: Harvard University Press, 2011).

14. Gerald David Jaynes et al., *A Common Destiny: Blacks and American Society* (Washington, D.C.: National Academy Press, 1989); Marc Mauer and Tracy Huling, *Young Black Americans and the Criminal Justice System: Five Years Later* (Sentencing Project, 1995).

15. John J. DiIulio, "Prison Reforms That Make Sense: [Final Edition]," *Daily Press*, October 22, 1989, sec. Outlook.

16. "Review & Outlook (Editorial): Cracking Down," *Wall Street Journal, Eastern Edition*, August 10, 1989.

17. Clarence Page, "NAACP, Right-Wing Foes Get Friendly—Chicago Tribune," *Chicago Tribune*, April 13, 2011, http://articles.chicagotribune.com/2011-04-13/news/ct-oped-0413-page-20110413_1_naacp-prisons-drug-czar; Saki Knafo, "Rand Paul Decries Mandatory Minimum Sentences, Likens War on Drugs to Jim Crow," *Huffington Post*, September 18, 2013, http://www.huffingtonpost.com/2013/09/18/rand-paul-mandatory-minimum-laws_n_3949415.html; *Anderson Cooper Hears Newt Gingrich Talk About Improving Prisons and Asks "Who Are You?,"* 2013, http://www.youtube.com/watch?v=rrh75DSfsog&feature=youtube_gdata_player

18. Roy Wenzl, "Charles Koch's Views on Criminal Justice System Just May Surprise You," *The Wichita Eagle*, December 27, 2014, http://www.kansas.com/news/special-reports/koch/article5050731.html.

19. Cohen et al., "Bridging the Partisan Divide," Kahan, "Ideology, Motivated Reasoning, and Cognitive Reflection"; Nickerson, "Confirmation Bias"; Taber and Lodge, "Motivated Skepticism."

20. Cohen, "Party Over Policy."

21. Taber and Lodge, "Motivated Skepticism in the Evaluation of Political Beliefs" ; Dan M. Kahan, "Ideology, Motivated Reasoning, and Cognitive Reflection: An Experimental Study," SSRN Scholarly Paper (Rochester, NY: Social Science Research Network, November 29, 2012), http://papers.ssrn.com/abstract=2182588.

22. Richard F. West, Russell J. Meserve, and Keith E. Stanovich, "Cognitive Sophistication Does Not Attenuate the Bias Blind Spot," *Journal of Personality and Social Psychology* 103, no. 3 (September 2012): 506–19, doi:10.1037/a0028857.

23. Larry M. Bartels, "Beyond the Running Tally: Partisan Bias in Political Perceptions," *Political Behavior*, Special Issue: Parties and Partisanship, Part One, 24, no. 2 (June 2002): 117–50.

24. A good summary can be found in Michael Barber and Nolan McCarty, "Causes and Consequences of Polarization," in *Solutions to Political Polarization in America*, ed. Nathaniel Persily (Cambridge: Cambridge University Press, 2015).

25. Marc J. Hetherington and Jonathan D. Weiler, *Authoritarianism and Polarization in American Politics* (Cambridge: Cambridge University Press, 2009).

26. Jeffrey M. Berry and Sarah Sobieraj, *The Outrage Industry: Political Opinion Media and the New Incivility* (Oxford: Oxford University Press, 2013).

27. Theda Skocpol, "Naming the Problem: What It Will Take to Counter Extremism and Engage Americans in the Fight against Global Warming," Symposium on the Politics of America's Fight Against Global Warming (Harvard University, January 2013), http://www.scholarsstrategynetwork.org/sites/default/files/skocpol_captrade_report_january_2013_0.pdf.

28. Barber and McCarty, "Causes and Consequences of Polarization."

29. Frances Lee, "Making Deals in Congress," in *Solutions to Political Polarization in America*, ed. Nathaniel Persily (Cambridge: Cambridge University Press, 2015).

30. Kahan et al., "Who Fears the HPV Vaccine, Who Doesn't, and Why?"

31. Braman, Kahan, and Grimmelmann, "The Gun Debate."

32. Glenn Loury has argued that a similar process structures the conditions under which criticisms of existing policy are considered acceptable (for example, a black person criticizing affirmative action is viewed as likely to possess real information, as opposed to a white person who will immediately be suspected as being motivated by racism). Glenn C. Loury, "Self-Censorship in Public Discourse: A Theory of 'Political Correctness' and Related Phenomena," *Rationality and Society* 6, no. 4 (October 1, 1994): 428–61, doi:10.1177/1043463194006004002.

33. Marshall Ganz, *Why David Sometimes Wins: Leadership, Organization, and Strategy in the California Farm Worker Movement* (Oxford: Oxford University Press, 2010), 11.

34. The classic account of the creation and disruption of policy images is Frank R. Baumgartner and Bryan D. Jones, *Agendas and Instability in American Politics* (Chicago: University of Chicago Press, 1993). Accounts of the psychology of stable group beliefs and their destabilization that more or less comport with the account in Baumgartner and Jones can be found in Arie W. Kruglanski, *The Psychology of Closed Mindedness* (New York: Psychology Press, 2013); Kurt Lewin, "Group Decisions and Social Change," in *Readings in Social Psychology* (New York: Holt, 1952), 459–73; Robert B. Zajonc and Julian Morrissette, "The Role of Uncertainty in Cognitive Change," *Journal of Abnormal and Social Psychology* 61, no. 2 (1960): 168–75.

35. On policy cascades, see Frank Baugmartner and Bryan Jones, *The Politics of Attention: How Government Prioritizes Problems* (Chicago: University of Chicago Press, 2005), pp. 140–142.

36. David Karol, *Party Position Change in American Politics: Coalition Management* (Cambridge: Cambridge University Press, 2009).

37. Ibid., 17.

Chapter 2

1. James Q. Wilson, "A Guide to Reagan Country: The Political Culture of Southern California," *Commentary* 43, no 5 (May 1, 1967).
2. Pat Nolan, interview, April 17, 2015.
3. Ibid.
4. Lisa McGirr, *Suburban Warriors: The Origins of the New American Right* (Princeton: Princeton University Press, 2002).
5. Ibid.
6. Greg Lucas, "Assemblyman Pleads Guilty to Racketeering," *The San Francisco Chronicle*, February 19, 1994.
7. Claudia Buck, "GOP Assemblyman Dishes Out Laughs, Ulcers in Fast Power Rise," *Sacramento Bee*, December 23, 1984.
8. Nolan, interview, April 17, 2015.
9. "California: Past Governors Bios," *National Governors Association*, accessed July 19, 2015, http://www.nga.org/cms/home/governors/past-governors-bios/page_california.default.html?beginbb1050a0-731b-4727-8048-a50a5584eadd=0&&pagesizebb1050a0-731b-4727-8048-a50a5584eadd=100.
10. Pat Nolan, interview, March 1, 2012.
11. Samuel Lubell, *The Future of American Politics* (New York: Doubleday, 1956).
12. Joseph Crespino, *Strom Thurmond's America*, Reprint edition (New York: Hill and Wang, 2013).
13. Numerous recent works have argued for the similarity of Northern and Southern responses to desegregation and integration, and the ways they simultaneously weakened white attachment to the Democratic Party and led to suburbanization, including Kevin Kruse, *White Flight: Atlanta and the Making of Modern Conservatism* (Princeton, NJ: Princeton University Press, 2007); Thomas Sugrue, *The Origins of the Urban Crisis: Race and Inequality in Postwar Detroit* (Princeton, NJ: Princeton University Press, 1996); Ron Formisano, *Boston Against Busing: Race, Class and Ethnicity in the 1960s and 1970s* (Chapel Hill: University of North Carolina, 1991).
14. Donald Alexander Downs, *Cornell '69: Liberalism and the Crisis of the American University*, 1st ed. (Ithaca, NY: Cornell University Press, 1999).

15. Rick Perlstein, *The Invisible Bridge: The Fall of Nixon and the Rise of Reagan* (New York: Simon and Schuster, 2014), 505, 609; William Graebner, *Patty's Got a Gun: Patricia Hearst in 1970s America*, 1st ed. (Chicago: University of Chicago Press, 2008).

16. On the reliability of violent-crime data, see Vesla M. Weaver, "Frontlash: Race and the Development of Punitive Crime Policy," *Studies in American Political Development* 21, no. 2 (2007): 230–65, doi:10.1017/S0898588X07000211. For a more detailed discussion of homicides, see Lisa L. Miller, *The Myth of Mob Rule: Violent Crime and Democratic Politics* (Oxford: Oxford University Press, 2016).

17. Quoted in Vesla M. Weaver, "Frontlash: Race and the Development of Punitive Crime Policy."

18. Steve Macek, *Urban Nightmares: The Media, the Right, and the Moral Panic over the City* (Minneapolis: University of Minnesota Press, 2006).

19. *Death Wish*, dir. Michael Winner, USA, Paramount, 1974; *Dirty Harry*, dir. Don Siegel, USA, Warner, 1971.

20. Naomi Murakawa, *The First Civil Right: How Liberals Built Prison America* (Oxford: Oxford University Press, 2014), 34–36.

21. Ibid., 60.

22. For more on Goldwater's campaign rhetoric, see Rick Perlstein, *Before the Storm: Barry Goldwater and the Unmaking of the American Consensus* (New York: Hill and Wang, 2001), 214, 422–26, 431–32, 460–61, 482–87.

23. Murakawa, *The First Civil Right: How Liberals Built Prison America*, 76.

24. Charles Mohr, "Goldwater Links the Welfare State to Rise in Crime," *The New York Times*, September 11, 1964, http://www.nytimes.com/1964/09/11/goldwater-links-the-welfare-state-to-rise-in-crime.html.

25. Richard Nixon, "Address Accepting the Presidential Nomination at the Republican National Convention in Miami Beach, Florida," August 8, 1968, http://www.presidency.ucsb.edu/ws/?pid=25968.

26. Ibid.

27. Tali Mendelberg, *The Race Card: Campaign Strategy, Implicit Messages, and the Norm of Equality* (Princeton, NJ: Princeton University Press, 2001), 4.

28. Harry R. Haldeman, *The Haldeman Diaries: Inside the Nixon White House* (New York: Berkley Books, 1994). See also: "Haldeman Diary Shows Nixon Was Wary of Blacks and Jews," *The New York Times*, May 18, 1994, sec. U.S., http://www. nytimes.com/1994/05/18/us/haldeman-diary-shows-nixon-was-wary-of-blacks-and-jews.html.

29. Perlstein, *The Invisible Bridge*, 88.

30. Carton E. Turner and Patricia Schroeder, "Should Employees Be Tested for Drug Use?," *The Telegraph*, April 13, 1986.

31. Naomi Murakawa, *Electing to Punish: Congress, Race, and the American Criminal Justice State* (PhD diss., Yale University, 2005), 72.

32. Ronald Reagan, "Remarks Announcing Federal Initiatives Against Drug Trafficking and Organized Crime" (Department of Justice, October 14, 1982), http://www.reagan.utexas.edu/archives/speeches/1982/101482c.htm.

33. The long-standing argument that contemporary liberalism represents a coalition of the affluent and the poor against the middle class has most recently been made in Fred Siegel, *The Revolt Against the Masses: How Liberalism Has Undermined the Middle Class* (New York: Encounter, 2014).

34. A version of this argument can be found in Rick Perlstein, *Nixonland* (New York: Scribner, 2009).

35. On the idea that the Democrats were becoming a party of "dangerous classes" aligned with a professional "New Class," see the contributions to B. Bruce Briggs, *The New Class?* (New Brunswick, NJ: Transaction, 1979), especially Norman Podhoretz, "The New Class and Adversary Culture."

36. Murakawa, *The First Civil Right: How Liberals Built Prison America*; Michael Fortner, *Black Silent Majority: The Rockefeller Drug Laws and the Politics of Punishment* (Cambridge, MA: Harvard University Press, 2015).

37. Kevin J. Smant, *Principles and Heresies: Frank S. Meyer and the Shaping of the American Conservative Movement*, 1st ed. (Wilmington, DE: ISI Books, 2002).

38. The classic version of this is "Nonmarket Decision Making: The Peculiar Economics of Bureaucracy," *American Economic Review* 58, no. 2 (May 1968): 294–305.

39. Jeffrey Henig, "Education Policy from 1980 to Present: The Politics of Privatization," in Steven Teles and Brian Glenn, *Conservatism and American Political Development* (Oxford: Oxford University Press, 2009), 291–323.

40. Daniel T. Rodgers, "'Moocher Class' Warfare," *Democracy: A Journal of Ideas* 24 (Spring 2012): 84.

41. Dan Baum, *Smoke and Mirrors: The War on Drugs and the Politics of Failure* (Boston: Back Bay Books, 1997), 137.

42. "The Vision Shared: Republican Party Platform of 1992," August 17, 1992, http://www.presidency.ucsb.edu/ws/ ?pid=25847. The instinct to rally around all the defenders of order remains strong: GOP presidential candidate Chris Christie in 2015 declared, "When the President of the United States doesn't back up law enforcement officers in uniform, he loses the moral authority to [lead] any man or woman who is in uniform." *New York Times*, "Transcript: G.O.P. Presidential Undercard Featuring Jindal and Huckabee," *New York Times*, November 10, 2015, http://www.nytimes.com/2015/11/11/us/ politics/transcript-gop-presidential-undercard-featuring-chris- tie-and-huckabee.html.

43. Joshua Page, *The Toughest Beat: Politics, Punishment, and the Prison Officers Union in California*, Reprint (New York: Oxford University Press, 2013).

44. John J. DiIulio, *Governing Prisons* (New York: Simon and Schuster, 1990).

45. The classic version of the argument that rehabilitation does not work was Robert Martinson, "What Works?—Questions and Answers About Prison Reform," *The Public Interest*, Spring 1974, 22–54.

46. James Wilson, *Thinking About Crime* (New York: Basic Books, 2013).

47. Isa. 18:2, New International Version, http://biblehub.com/niv/ isaiah/32.htm.

48. Nolan, interview, April 17, 2015.

Chapter 3

1. Julie Stewart, "Sentencing in the States: The Good, the Bad, and the Ugly," *Osgoode Hall Law Journal* 39, no. 2/3 (Summer/Fall 2001): 414. See also "FAMM: Julie Stewart, President and Founder," accessed June 10, 2015, http://famm.org/about/board-and-staff/julie-stewart/.

2. Stephen Chapman, "A 'Safety Valve' to Ease Pressures Is a Good Start," *The Chicago Tribune*, August 4, 1994, http://articles.chicagotribune.com/1994-08-04/news/9408040050_1_drug-offenders-drug-war-federal-prison; "Safety Valves," *FAMM*, accessed June 10, 2015, http://famm.org/projects/federal/us-congress/safety-valves/.

3. David Boaz, the vice president of the Cato Institute, observes that "Politically, 'libertarianism with a small 'l' was very skeptical of Republicanism with a capital 'R,' but they were bound by their mutual abhorrence of communism and the welfare state." Karen Tumulty, "Libertarians Flex Their Muscle in the GOP," *The Washington Post*, July 31, 2013.

4. William J. Stuntz, "Law and Grace," *Virginia Law Review* 98 (2012): 367; William J. Stuntz, "Race, Class, and Drugs," *Columbia Law Review* 98, no. 7 (November 1, 1998): 1795–842; William J. Stuntz, "The Uneasy Relationship between Criminal Procedure and Criminal Justice," *The Yale Law Journal* 107, no. 1 (October 1, 1997): 1–76.

5. Julie Stewart, interview, July 10, 2012.

6. David B. Holian, "He's Stealing My Issues! Clinton's Crime Rhetoric and the Dynamics of Issue Ownership," *Political Behavior* 26, no. 2 (June 2004).

7. Ron Faucheux, "Going into 2000, Democrats Have an Issue Edge," *Campaigns and Elections* 20, no. 10 (December 1999): 7.

8. Lisa Miller shows that public, media, and political attention to crime correlates significantly to rates of violent crime in Lisa L. Miller, *The Myth of Mob Rule: Violent Crime and Democratic Politics* (Oxford: Oxford University Press, 2016).

9. On Texas, for example, see: Michael C. Campbell, "Agents of Change: Law Enforcement, Prisons, and Politics in Texas and California" (Ph.D., University of California, Irvine, 2009);

Sean Cunningham, *Cowboy Conservatism: Texas and the Rise of the Modern Right* (Lexington: University Press of Kentucky, 2010); Robert Perkinson, *Texas Tough: The Rise of America's Prison Empire* (New York, NY: Macmillan, 2010).

10. Almost, but not complete. Virginia, for instance, is very closely contested in national and gubernatorial elections, and it has a very narrow Republican majority in the state Senate. As we argue in the conclusion, this helps explain why Republicans in the state have held on so tightly to 1980s-era crime rhetoric. Republicans at the state level are less willing to surrender the crime issue, even at its lower level of current potency, when their hold on power is tenuous. This may also go a ways toward explaining the lesser enthusiasm for criminal justice reform in states like Washington (where Republicans hold a bare majority in the state Senate and are a minority in the House).

11. Peverill Squire and Keith E. Hamm, *One Hundred and One Chambers* (Columbus, OH: Ohio State University Press, 2005), 142.

12. Ryan S. King and Marc Mauer, "State Sentencing and Corrections Policy in an Era of Fiscal Restraint" (Washington, D.C.: The Sentencing Project, February 2002), http://www.sentencingproject.org/doc/publications/inc_statesentencingpolicy.pdf; Ryan S. King, "Changing Direction? State Sentencing Reforms, 2004-2006" (Washington, D.C.: The Sentencing Project, March 2007), http://www.sentencingproject.org/doc/publications/sentencingreformforweb.pdf; Judith Greene, "Cutting Correctly: New Prison Policies for Times of Fiscal Crisis" (San Francisco: Center on Juvenile and Criminal Justice, 2001), http://www.cjcj.org/files/cut_cor.pdf.

13. "Right-Sizing Prisons: Business Leaders Make the Case for Corrections Reform" (Washington, DC: The Pew Center on the States, January 2010), http://www.pewcenteronthestates.org/report_detail.aspx?id=56721.

14. Marie Gottschalk, "Cell Blocks & Red Ink: Mass Incarceration, the Great Recession & Penal Reform," *Daedalus* 139, no. 3 (July 1, 2010): 62–73, doi:10.1162/DAED_a_00023.

15. Jack Bascom Brooks, "Comprehensive Crime Control Act of 1990," Report on Public Bill, 14017 H.rp.681/1 (House Committee on the Judiciary, September 5, 1990), 77; Stephen Wermiel, "U.S. Sentencing Proposals Spur Worries over Inmate Rise, Cost of New Prisons," *Wall Street Journal, Eastern Edition*, June 22, 1987; White, "The Illogical Lockup: [3 Star Edition]," *Orlando Sentinel*, April 27, 1987, sec. Editorial Page; Dave McNeely, "Key Legislators Question Borrowing for Prison Construction: [Final Edition]," *Austin American Statesman*, January 19, 1989, sec. City/State; David Poulson and Grand Rapids Press Bureau, "Officials, Taxpayers Struggle with Fiscal Drain of Prisons," *The Grand Rapids Press*, February 16, 1992; Stuart Taylor Jr., "Strict Penalties for Criminals: Pendulum of Feeling Swings," *New York Times, Late Edition (East Coast)*, December 13, 1983, sec. A; Adam Yeomans, "Senate Leader Backs Stop Bill," *Tallahassee Democrat*, January 11, 1995; Michael C. Campbell and Heather Schoenfeld, "The Transformation of America's Penal Order: A Historicized Political Sociology of Punishment," *American Journal of Sociology* 118, no. 5 (March 2013): 1375–423.

16. "Prison Count 2010" (Washington, D.C.: The Pew Center on the States, April 2010), http://www.pewcenteronthestates.org/ uploadedFiles/Prison_Count_2010.pdf.

17. Christy Hoppe, "Extra $1.5 Billion Not Exactly a Surplus: Texas Legislators Earmarked Much of the Increased Funds," *The Dallas Morning News*, October 10, 2007, sec. 3A.

18. Recent work supports the claim that the role of economics and partisanship on incarceration is mixed. Phelps and Pager found no correlation between a measure of state fiscal capacity and incarceration rates in the 1980s and 1990s. They find a marginally significant correlation in the 2000s and a statistically significant correlation beginning after 2010. On partisanship, Phelps and Pager find Republican power is associated with higher incarceration rates in recent years, whereas Campbell and his co-authors find no such relationship. See Michelle S. Phelps and Devah Pager, "Inequality and Punishment: A Turning Point for Mass Incarceration?," *The ANNALS of the*

American Academy of Political and Social Science 663, no. 1 (January 1, 2016): 185–203; Michael C. Campbell, Matt Vogel, and Joshua Williams, "Historical Contingencies and the Evolving Importance of Race, Violent Crime, and Region in Explaining Mass Incarceration in the United States," *Criminology* 53, no. 2 (May 1, 2015): 180–203.

19. Ryan S. King and Marc Mauer, "State Sentencing and Corrections Policy in an Era of Fiscal Restraint"; Ryan S. King, "Changing Direction? State Sentencing Reforms, 2004–2006"; Judith Greene, "Cutting Correctly: New Prison Policies for Times of Fiscal Crisis."

Chapter 4

1. For a review of incarceration rates by education level, see Bruce Western and Jeremy Travis, eds., *The Growth of Incarceration in the United States: Exploring Causes and Consequences* (Washington, D.C.: The National Academies Press, 2014), 65.

2. Robert B. Gunnison and Greg Lucas, "Jury Indicts 2 Legislators in Sting Case," *The San Francisco Chronicle*, April 28, 1993.

3. K. L. Billingsley, "FBI Sting against Calif. GOP Leader Termed Corrupt," *The Washington Times*, October 12, 1993.

4. Ibid.

5. Greg Lucas, "Assemblyman Pleads Guilty to Racketeering," *The San Francisco Chronicle*, February 19, 1994.

6. "Pat Nolan Begins Bribery Prison Term," *The San Francisco Chronicle*, April 5, 1994.

7. Pat Nolan, interview, July 20, 2015.

8. Pat Nolan, interview, March 1, 2012.

9. Charles W. Colson, *Life Sentence* (Grand Rapids, MI: Fleming H. Revell, 1979), 14–16. A total of 43 people died as a result of the raid.

10. Ibid., 14.

11. Ibid., 15.

12. Ibid. The actual number of dead inmates appears to have been 28. *Attica: The Official Report of the New York State Special Commission on Attica* (New York: Bantam, 1972), p. 458.

13. Charles W. Colson, *Born Again* (Grand Rapids, MI: Chosen Books, 2008).

14. "Fact Sheet: Prison Fellowship," accessed November 16, 2015, http://demoss.com/newsrooms/pf/background/prison-fellowship-fact-sheet.

15. "Timeline: History of Prison Fellowship," accessed November 16, 2015, http://demoss.com/newsrooms/pf/background/timeline-history-of-prison-fellowship.

16. Glenn Loury, interview, July 10, 2015.

17. Ibid.

18. Ibid.

19. Comments from Christian Coalition founder Ralph Reed and Focus on the Family President and CEO Jim Daly posted on "Tributes," *Chuck Colson Legacy Fund*, accessed May 25, 2014, http://chuckcolson.org/tributes.

20. John J. DiIulio, interview, July 3, 2015.

21. Loury, interview.

22. Frank Wolf, interview, July 20, 2015.

23. Charles W. Colson, "The End of Democracy? Kingdoms in Conflict," *First Things*, November 1996, http://www.firstthings.com/article/1996/11/006-the-end-of-democracy-kingdoms-in-conflict.

24. DiIulio, interview.

25. Ibid.

26. Michael J. Gerson, "Heroic Conservatism: Why Republicans Need to Embrace America's Ideals (And Why They Deserve to Fail If They Don't)," *Commentary* 125, no. 1 (2008): 31.

27. Frank Wolf, interview, July 20, 2015.

28. Ibid.

29. *Congressional Record*, May 15, 2012.

30. *Congressional Record*, May 16, 2012.

31. Tim Dunn, interview, March 2, 2012.

32. Matt Sledge, "California Prison Reform's Biggest Backer Is Also Friends with Karl Rove," *The Huffington Post*, October 2, 2014, http://www.huffingtonpost.com/2014/10/02/b-wayne-hughes-jr-prison-reform_n_5915568.html.

33. Katia Savchuk, "Why a Conservative Billionaire Is Backing Criminal Justice Reform in California," *Forbes*, October 30, 2014, http://www.forbes.com/sites/katiasavchuk/2014/10/30/why-a-conservative-billionaire-wants-to-reduce-sentences-for-drug-and-theft-crimes-in-california/.

34. Richard Land, interview, September 27, 2012.
35. Kent R. Kerley et al., "From the Sanctuary to the Slammer: Exploring the Narratives of Evangelical Prison Ministry Workers," *Sociological Spectrum* 30, no. 5 (2010): 504–25.
36. Ibid., 514.
37. DiIulio, interview.
38. Nolan, interview, July 20, 2015.
39. The Chuck Colson Center for Christian Worldview, "About Chuck Colson (1931–2012)," accessed May 25, 2014, http://www.colsoncenter.org/the-center/the-chuck-colson-center/about-chuck-colson; Jonathan Aitken, *Charles W. Colson: A Life Redeemed* (New York: Crown Publishing Group, 2010), 319–20.
40. Julie Stewart, interview, July 10, 2012.
41. Pat Nolan, interview, July 22, 2015.
42. Pat Nolan, interview, April 19, 2011.
43. Virginia Sloan, interview, July 10, 2015.
44. Ibid.
45. David Keene, interview, March 5, 2012.
46. David Keene, "An Odd Coalition Is Fighting Asset Forfeiture," *The Hill*, May 5, 1999.
47. David Keene, "Conservatives Must Protect the People's Civil Rights," *The Hill*, March 3, 1999.
48. Sloan, interview.
49. Richard Viguerie, interview, March 13, 2012.
50. David Keene, interview, May 9, 2014.
51. Pat Nolan, interview, June 18, 2015.
52. David Keene, interview, March 5, 2012; Craig Gilbert, "NRA Chief Defies Stereotype: David Keene Isn't Militaristic About Pro-Gun Message, But Says He's Always Ready for a Fight," *Newport News*, March 3, 2013, sec. A.
53. James A. Strazzella, "Task Force on the Federalization of Criminal Law" (Washington, D.C.: American Bar Association, Criminal Justice Section, 1998).
54. Paul Rosenzweig and Brian W. Walsh, *One Nation Under Arrest: How Crazy Laws, Rogue Prosecutors, and Activist Judges Threaten Your Liberty* (Washington, D.C.: The Heritage Foundation, 2010).
55. Pat Nolan, interview, July 8, 2015.
56. Ibid.

57. Herbert J. Hoelter, "Criminal Defense Update: On Death and Dying in the Federal Bureau of Prisons—The Recent Report from the Office of the Inspector General" (NCIA, May 2013), http://www.ncianet.org/wp-content/uploads/2015/03/On-Death-and-Dying-May-2013.pdf.

58. Sloan, interview.

59. Galen Carey, interview, September 28, 2012.

60. Land, interview.

61. Tony Perkins, interview, July 12, 2012.

62. Ibid.

63. Thomas Medvetz, "The Strength of Weekly Ties: Relations of Material and Symbolic Exchange in the Conservative Movement," *Politics & Society* 34, no. 3 (September 1, 2006): 343–68.

64. Grover Norquist, "Making Crime Pay," *American Spectator* 26, no. 5 (May 1993): 44.

65. Norquist, "Making Crime Pay."

66. Julie Stewart, interview, March 31, 2014.

67. Grover Norquist, interview, March 19, 2014.

68. Ibid.

69. Ibid.

70. Nolan, interview, June 18, 2015; Pat Nolan, interview, June 26, 2014.

71. Nolan, interview, April 19, 2011.

72. Ibid.; David Keene, interview, March 5, 2012.

73. Jessica Collins and Katherine Rexrode, "House Judiciary Committee Announces Criminal Justice Reform Initiative," *US House of Representatives Judiciary Committee,* June 10, 2015, http://www.judiciary.house.gov/index.cfm/press-releases?id=9A79947D-9FFF-4DF8-B133-8E27B5E92394.

74. Nolan, interview, June 18, 2015.

75. David Keene, interview, May 9, 2014.

76. *Anderson Cooper Hears Newt Gingrich Talk About Improving Prisons and Asks "Who Are You?,"* 2013, http://www.youtube.com/watch?v=rrh75DSfsog&feature=youtube_gdata_player.

77. Newt Gingrich, interview, February 18, 2014.

78. Michael C. Campbell and Heather Schoenfeld, "The Transformation of America's Penal Order: A Historicized Political Sociology of Punishment," *American Journal of Sociology* 118, no. 5 (March 2013): 1375–423.

Chapter 5

1. John W. Kingdon, *Agendas, Alternatives and Public Policies* (Boston: Little, Brown, 1984).
2. Email from Eric Cadora, June 27, 2015.
3. Eric Cadora, interview, January 27, 2015.
4. Ryan J. Reilly, "The Civil Rights Chief DOJ Thinks Liberals Will Love, Conservatives Can Work With," *The Huffington Post*, October 10, 2014, http://www.huffingtonpost.com/ 2014/10/15/vanita-gupta-doj-civil-rights-ferguson_n_ 5993310.html; U.S. Programs, "OSF Awards More than $1.25 Million Nationwide to New Leaders in Criminal Justice Reform," *Open Society Foundations*, January 31, 2005, http:// www.opensocietyfoundations.org/press-releases/OSF- awards-more-125-million-nationwide-new-leaders-criminal- justice-reform.
5. Franklin E. Zimring and Gordon J. Hawkins, *The Scale of Imprisonment* (Chicago: University of Chicago Press, 1993), 211.
6. Susan Tucker and Eric Cadora, "Justice Reinvestment: To Invest in Public Safety by Reallocating Justice Dollars to Refinance Education, Housing, Healthcare, and Jobs," Ideas for an Open Society (New York: Open Society Institute, November 2003), http://bit.ly/1B9aAdA.
7. Cadora, interview.
8. Tucker and Cadora, "Justice Reinvestment: To Invest in Public Safety by Reallocating Justice Dollars to Refinance Education, Housing, Healthcare, and Jobs."
9. Ibid., 2.
10. Cadora, interview.
11. Gara LaMarche, interview, January 7, 2015.
12. Founded in 1933, CSG is a nonprofit that aims to help officials from all three branches of government work across state lines. It runs bipartisan brainstorming sessions and teaches leadership skills, negotiates interstate compacts, and advises states on inter- actions with the federal government, among other activities. "About CSG," accessed January 21, 2016, http://www.csg.org/ about/.
13. Email from Michael Thompson, June 23, 2015.
14. Michael Thompson, interview, January 6, 2015.

15. Michael Thompson, "Corrections and the State Budget Crises: Fiscal and Public Safety Implications:—A Strategy Paper Making the Case for Targeted Federal Assistance," n.d.

16. Email from Thompson, June 23, 2015.

17. Michael Thompson, "Presentation to the Connecticut Appropriations and Judiciary Committees" (Council of State Governments Justice Center, April 22, 2014), http://csgjustice-center.org/jr/connecticut/publications/presentation-to-the-connecticut-appropriations-and-judiciary-committees/; "Building Bridges: From Conviction to Employment: One Year Later" (Council of State Governments Criminal Justice Programs, February 18, 2004), http://csgjusticecenter.org/jr/connecticut/publications/building-bridges-from-conviction-to-employment-one-year-later/; Thompson, interview, January 6, 2015.

18. Connecticut General Assembly Office of Fiscal Analysis, "Connecticut State Budget, 2003-2005," n.d., 302–03, http://1.usa.gov/1I6G1sa.

19. Ibid.

20. Ibid.; Thompson, "Presentation to the Connecticut Appropriations and Judiciary Committees"; Michael Thompson, interview, January 6, 2015.

21. Cadora, interview.

22. Ibid.

23. Thompson, interview, January 6, 2015.

24. Michael Thompson, interview, July 24, 2015.

25. Michael Thompson, interview, February 19, 2015.

26. Ibid.

27. "TPPF: Reduce Drug Sentences, Strengthen Probation to Avert Texas' Overincarceration Crisis," *Grits for Breakfast*, May 25, 2006, http://gritsforbreakfast.blogspot.com/2006/05/tppf-reduce-drug-sentences-strengthen.html.

28. Lori Grange, interview, January 13, 2015; Adam Gelb, interview, January 7, 2015; "Public Safety Performance: Protecting Public Safety, Holding Offenders Accountable, Controlling Corrections Costs" (Pew Charitable Trusts, n.d.).

29. Grange, interview, January 13, 2015.

30. Thompson, interview, February 19, 2015.

31. Grange, interview, January 13, 2015.

32. "Public Safety Performance: Protecting Public Safety, Holding Offenders Accountable, Controlling Corrections Costs."

33. Gelb, interview, January 7, 2015.

34. Cadora, interview.

35. Thompson, interview, July 24, 2015.

36. Adam Gelb, interview, December 7, 2013.

37. Grange, interview, January 13, 2015.

38. Gelb, interview, January 7, 2015.

39. Thompson, interview, February 19, 2015.

40. Ibid.

Chapter 6

1. Arlette Saenz, "George Bush Executed Texans Faster Than Rick Perry," *ABC News*, September 22, 2011, http://abcnews. go.com/blogs/politics/2011/09/george-bush-executed-texans-at-faster-rate-than-rick-perry/.

2. Allen J. Beck and Paige M. Harrison, "Prisoners in 2000" (Bureau of Justice Statistics, August 2001), http://www.bjs.gov/content/pub/pdf/p00.pdf.

3. Sean Cunningham, *Cowboy Conservatism: Texas and the Rise of the Modern Right* (Lexington: University Press of Kentucky, 2010), 69.

4. Ibid, 38.

5. Ibid., 60–61.

6. Ibid., 78.

7. William Justice, Ruiz v. Estelle, 503 F.Sup. 1265 (1980). See "Prison Reform: Ruiz v. Estelle," *The William Wayne Justice Papers*, 2014, http://tarlton.law.utexas.edu/exhibits/ww_justice/ruiz_v_estelle.html; "Cruel and Unusual Punishment: Ruiz," *The Texas Politics Project*, n.d., http://texaspolitics.utexas.edu/archive/html/just/features/0505_01/ruiz.html; *Judicial Policy Making and the Modern State: How the Courts Reformed America's Prisons*, first paperback edition (Cambridge: Cambridge University Press, 2000), 85.

8. Sheldon Ekland-Olson et al., *Justice Under Pressure: A Comparison of Recidivism Patterns Among Four Successive Parolee Cohorts*, (New York: Springer, 1993); "Staff Evaluation: Texas Department of Corrections" (Texas Department of Corrections, September 1986), 42, https://www.sunset.texas.gov/public/

uploads/files/reports/Department%20of%20Corrections%20
%28TDCJ%29%20Staff%20Evaluation%201986%2070th%20Leg.
pdf.

9. Robert Perkinson, *Texas Tough: The Rise of America's Prison
Empire* (New York: Henry Holt and Co., 2010), 317; Michael
C. Campbell, "Agents of Change: Law Enforcement, Prisons,
and Politics in Texas and California" (PhD, University of
California, Irvine, 2009), 138–39.

10. Robert Perkinson, *Texas Tough: The Rise of America's Prison
Empire,* First Edition (New York: Henry Holt and Co., 2010),
319.

11. Laylan Copelin, "Richards Takes Her Campaign to Prison
Series: Campaign 1990: [Final Edition]," *Austin American
Statesman,* July 26, 1990, sec. City/State. Prison numbers via
email from Jeff Baldwin, Texas Department of Criminal Justice.

12. Perkinson, *Texas Tough,* 2010, 322.

13. Clay Robinson, "Election '91—Texans Resoundingly
Approve Prison Bonds," *Houston Chronicle,* November 6, 1991,
4 Star edition, sec. A News, 91; Diana R. Fuentes, "Richards
to Take Issues Push on Road," *San Antonio Express News,*
October 8, 1991; Christy Hoppe, "Separate Jail System Hits
Ballot—$1 Billion Would Pay to House the Nonviolent,"
Dallas Morning News, October 25, 1993, Home Final edition,
sec. News; Clay Robinson, "Election '93—Texans Giving
Nod to More Prisons, Mental Hospitals—Thumbs down on
Bonds for State Businesses," *Houston Chronicle,* November 3,
1993, 2 Star edition, sec. A News, 93.

14. Email from Jeff Baldwin.

15. Nate Blakeslee, "Hooked on Hard Time," *The Texas Observer,*
February 16, 2001, http://www.texasobserver.org/19-hooked-on-
hard-time-perrys-budget-feeds-the-prison-construction-industry-
while-drug-treatment-goes-hungry/; Tony Fabelo, March 30, 2015.

16. Perkinson, *Texas Tough,* 2010, 323–24.

17. Fox Butterfield, "On the Record: Governor Bush on Crime;
Bush's Law and Order Adds Up to Tough and Popular," *The
New York Times,* August 18, 1999, sec. U.S., http://www.
nytimes.com/1999/08/18/us/record-governor-bush-crime-
bush-s-law-order-adds-up-tough-popular.html.

18. Clay Robinson, "Painting into Corners on Texas Prisons," *Houston Chronicle*, February 2003.

19. Nate Blakeslee, "The Color of Justice," *The Texas Observer*, June 23, 2000, http://www.texasobserver.org/611-the-color-of-justice/.

20. Rebecca Leung, "Targeted in Tulia, Texas?," September 26, 2003, http://www.cbsnews.com/news/targeted-in-tulia-texas-26-09-2003/.

21. Lewis Beale, "Taking Drug Task Forces to Task: Film Takes a Look at the Unintended Consequences of One Weapon in the Arsenal Devoted to the War on Drugs," *Pacific Standard*, April 17, 2009, http://www.psmag.com/politics-and-law/taking-drug-task-forces-to-task-3794; Nate Blakeslee, "Bust Town," *Texas Monthly*, November 2002, http://www.texasmonthly.com/articles/bust-town/.

22. *Tulia Corroboration Bill*, 2001, http://www.capitol.state.tx.us/BillLookup/History.aspx?LegSess=77R&Bill= HB2351.

23. "Gov. Perry Pardons 35 Tulia Defendants," *CNN*, August 22, 2003, http://www.cnn.com/2003/LAW/08/22/tulia.pardons/index.html?eref=sitesearch.

24. Email from Scott Henson, March 24, 2015.

25. Polly Ross Hughes, "Perry's Prison Plan Questioned/Governor Budgets $95 Million for Lockups, Zero for Pay Raises: [3 Star Edition]," *Houston Chronicle*, January 17, 2001, sec. A.

26. Pat Haggerty, interview, March 24, 2015.

27. Ibid.

28. "Internal Solutions for Sentencing and Incarceration: Campaign Plan" (Texas Criminal Justice Coalition, n.d.).

29. S. C. Gwynne, "Tom Craddick," *Texas Monthly*, February 2005, http://www.texasmonthly.com/story/1-tom-craddick.

30. Jackie Calmes, "Bush's Home State Faces Budget 'Mess'—Tax Cuts Helped the Ex-Governor Win Presidency, but Now Texas Has to Pay the Piper," *Wall Street Journal, Eastern Edition*, January 22, 2003, sec. Politics & Policy.

31. Mike Ward, "Prisons Planning Hundreds of Layoffs; 600 Jobs Will Be Cut, but Workers May Sign on to Fill Guard Positions," *Austin American Statesman*, April 2, 2003.

32. Dave Harmon, "Prisons Nearing Capacity Yet Again; Solutions Include Paroling Prisoners, Relying on County Jails," *Austin American Statesman*, February 13, 2003.

33. Ibid.

34. Scott Henson, interview, June 16, 2015; Ray Allen, interview, July 13, 2015.

35. Henson, interview.

36. "TPPF: Reduce Drug Sentences, Strengthen Probation to Avert Texas' Overincarceration Crisis," *Grits for Breakfast*, May 25, 2006, http://gritsforbreakfast.blogspot.com/2006/05/tppf-reduce-drug-sentences-strengthen.html; *Relating to the Early Termination of Parole and Mandatory Supervision*, 2003, http://www.legis.state.tx.us/BillLookup/Text.aspx?LegSess=78R&Bill=HB2670; *Relating to the Imposition of Sanctions on a Defendant Who Violates a Condition of Community Supervision*, 2003, http://www.legis.state.tx.us/BillLookup/History.aspx?LegSess=78R&Bill=HB2672; Scott Henson to David Dagan, July 9, 2015.

37. Perkinson, *Texas Tough*, 2010, 344.

38. Danny Kruger, "Why Texas Is Closing Prisons in Favour of Rehab," *BBC News*, December 1, 2014, http://www.bbc.com/news/world-us-canada-30275026.

39. Christopher Lee, "GOP Showdown Nears for Legislative Seat—Primary Likely to End Battle for Newly Drawn State House District 67," *The Dallas Morning News*, March 6, 1992, Home Final edition, sec. Plano. See also: "Jerry Madden," *The Dallas Morning News*, March 8, 1992, Home Final edition, sec. Special; "Jerry Madden," *The Dallas Morning News*, March 1, 2002, Second edition, sec. Plano Morning News.

40. "Biography," *Jerry Madden*, accessed May 26, 2015, http://jerrymadden.org/biography.html.

41. Wendy Hundley, "Ex-Plano Council Member Sets Sights on House Seat—Roach to Challenge Longtime Incumbent Madden in District 67," September 14, 2001, Third edition, sec. Metro.

42. John Young, "Texas Textbook Nexus; Political Forces Back Trying to Control Content to Their Liking," *Waco Tribune-Herald*, April 20, 2003; Robert T. Garrett, "House Panel Unveils Its 'Hot Button' Proposals—Ban on Gay Marriage, Abortion Restrictions Among Interim Plans," *Dallas Morning News*, December 17, 2004.

43. John O'Brien et al., "Adult and Juvenile Correctional Population Projections Fiscal Years 2005–2010" (Legislative Budget Board, January 2005), 6.

44. John Whitmire, interview, July 9, 2015.

45. Jay Root, "Senator John Whitmire Walks a Fine Line on Conflicts," *The New York Times*, January 17, 2013, http://www.nytimes.com/2013/01/18/us/senator-john-whitmire-walks-a-fine-line-on-conflicts.html. John Whitmire, "Texas Must Continue Being Tough on Crime," *The Dallas Morning News*, March 6, 1995; Reid Wilson, "Tough Texas Gets Results by Going Softer on Crime," *The Washington Post*, November 27, 2014, http://www.washingtonpost.com/blogs/govbeat/wp/2014/11/27/tough-texas-gets-results-by-going-softer-on-crime/.

46. Whitmire, "Texas Must Continue Being Tough on Crime."

47. Ibid.

48. Whitmire, interview.

49. Diane Jennings, "Full House—Growing Inmate Population Has Lawmakers Scrambling for Alternate Solutions," *The Dallas Morning News*, April 9, 2000.

50. Ibid.

51. Jerry Madden, interview, July 9, 2015.

52. Mike Ward, "Probation Overhaul Heads to Governor; If Perry Agrees, Some Felons' Time under Supervision Will Be Halved," *Austin American Statesman*, May 25, 2005.

53. Ward, "Prison Plan."

54. Mike Ward, "Probation Reform Savings Pegged—Senate Bill Analyses Show State Could Cut Costs by $49 Million," *Austin American-Statesman* (TX), May 6, 2005; Mike Ward, "Probation Reforms Flounder at Capitol—Opponents Say Bills Would Create More Prisoners, Not Fewer," *Austin American-Statesman* (TX), May 1, 2005.

55. House Research Organization, "Revising Probation/Community Supervision HB 2193 by Madden (Whitmire)," 2005; Mike Ward, "Probation Reforms Flounder at Capitol—Opponents Say Bills Would Create More Prisoners, Not Fewer."

56. Laylan Copelin, "House Approves Shorter Probation—Caps on Punishment Terms Seen as a Way to Concentrate Resources," *Austin American Statesman*, May 13, 2005, sec. Metro/State.

57. House Research Organization, "Revising Probation/ Community Supervision HB 2193 by Madden (Whitmire)."

58. Gritsforbreakfast, "Silver Linings: Probation Strengthening Measures Perry DIDN'T Veto," *Grits for Breakfast*, August 27, 2005, http://gritsforbreakfast.blogspot.com/2005/08/ silver-linings-probation-strengthening.html; House Research Organization, "Revising Probation/Community Supervision HB 2193 by Madden (Whitmire)."

59. House Research Organization, "Revising Probation/ Community Supervision HB 2193 by Madden (Whitmire)."

60. Fabelo, interview.

61. "Justice Reinvestment Texas: A Case Study" (Justice Center: The Council of State Governments, n.d.).

62. "Justice Reinvestment Texas: A Case Study", fig. 7.

63. Madden, interview.

64. Rick Perry, "State-of-the-State Address," February 6, 2007, 8, http://www.aclutx.org/files/070206PerrySoSaddress.pdf.

65. "Public Policy: Initiatives (Texas Passes Child Welfare Reforms and Expands Nurse Home Visiting Program in 2007)," accessed July 26, 2015, http://policy.db.zerotothree.org/policyp/view. aspx?InitiativeID=614&origin=results&QS=%27&union=AN D&viewby=50&startrec=1&tbl_Public_InitiativeYMGHFRE Category=Child+Welfare&top_parent=164; Stephen Carter, "Overlooked Texas Bill Allows Police to Cite and Release for Pot Possession, Will Counties Take Advantage to Ease Jail Costs?," *Texas Cannabis Report*, accessed July 26, 2015, http:// txcann.com/2013/09/24/texas-marijuana-bill-hb2391/.

66. John Whitmire, interview, March 8, 2012.

67. George Zornick, "Rick Perry at CPAC Panel on Criminal Justice: 'Shut Prisons Down. Save That Money,'" *The Nation*, March 7, 2014, http://www.thenation.com/article/rick-perry- cpac-panel-criminal-justice-shut-prisons-down-save-money/.

68. Nate Blakeslee, "Why Fewer Prisons Are Good for Texas's Economy," *Texas Monthly*, March 11, 2014, http://www. texasmonthly.com/politics/why-fewer-prisons-are-good- for-texass-economy/; *Relating to Certain Criminal Offenses, Punishments, and Procedures; the Construction of Certain Statutes and Rules That Create or Define Criminal Offenses and Penalties; a Review of Certain Penal Laws of This State*, 2015,

http://www.capitol.state.tx.us/BillLookup/History. aspx?LegSess=84R&Bill=HB1396; *Relating to the Award of Diligent Participation Credit to Defendants Confined in a State Jail Felony Facility,* 2011, http://www.capitol.state.tx.us/ BillLookup/History.aspx?LegSess=82R&Bill=HB2649; *Relating to Limiting the Liability of Persons Who Employ Persons with Criminal Convictions,* 2013, http://www.capitol.state.tx.us/ BillLookup/History.aspx?LegSess=83R& Bill=HB1188.

69. "Texas Smart-On-Crime Coalition—Smart on Crime in Texas," *Texas Smart-On-Crime Coalition,* accessed November 29, 2015, http://smartoncrimetexas.com/featured/ texas-smart-crime-coalition-tscc.

70. Email from Adam Gelb, June 4, 2012.

71. "Rep. Schiff Introduces Criminal Justice Reinvestment Act," *US Fed News Service, Including US State News,* November 20, 2009; Adam Schiff, *Criminal Justice Reinvestment Act of 2009, H.R. 4080 (2009–2010),* 2009. On Lungren's history, see Kate Stith and Steve Y. Koh, "Politics of Sentencing Reform: The Legislative History of the Federal Sentencing Guidelines," *Wake Forest Law Review* 28 (1993): 223.

72. Ian McCann, "Veteran Lawmaker Faced Tightest Race yet in GOP Primary—Madden Squeaks by with Narrow Victory in Southern Collin District," *Dallas Morning News,* March 6, 2008, South edition.

73. Kelley Chambers, "Madden Announces Retirement, 'Pinnacle of Achievement' after 19 Years," *Plano Star Courier* (TX), November 17, 2011.

Chapter 7

1. Eve Conant, "The GOP's Born-Again Prison Reformers," *The Daily Beast,* July 3, 2011, http://www.thedailybeast.com/articles/ 2011/07/03/gop-leaders-warm-up-to-prison-reform.html.

2. "Erick Erickson: Support Right on Crime," *Right on Crime,* 2014, http://rightoncrime.com/2014/08/erick-erickson-support-right-on-crime/.

3. Neena Satija, "TPFF Building the Foundation of Texas Conservatism," *The Texas Tribune,* January 7, 2015, http://www. texastribune.org/2015/01/07/tppf-moving-legislature-convenes/.

4. TPPF was cited by six members, or 23 percent of the sample. That made it the third most popular choice overall, after the Heritage Foundation and SPN generally.

5. David Mann, "Who Really Runs Texas?," *The Texas Observer*, October 2, 2012, http://www.texasobserver.org/who-really-runs-texas/.

6. Ashley May, "The Philanthropy Roundtable Goes to Prison," *Philanthropy Roundtable*, February 2013, http://www.philanthropyroundtable.org/topic/economic_opportunity/the_philanthropy_roundtable_goes_to_prison; email from Tim Dunn, July 15, 2015.

7. Tim Dunn, interview, March 2, 2012.

8. Jerry Madden, *Concurrent Resolution*, n.d., www.legis.state.tx.us/tlodocs/80R/billtext/doc/HC00251I.doc.

9. John J. Miller, "Fifty Flowers Bloom," *National Review*, November 19, 2007, http://www.heymiller.com/2009/09/fifty-flowers-bloom/.

10. Email from Marc A. Levin, July 28, 2015.

11. "Untitled Grant Application" (Center for Effective Justice, TPPF, n.d.), 13, 19.

12. Ibid., 13, 15.

13. "Rep. Madden Corrections Cost Containment Strategies at Annual National Conference of State Legislatures," *US Fed News Service, Including US State News*, August 12, 2009; Jamal Thalji, "Legislators Look West for Prison Solution: Texas Revamped Its Justice System instead of Building Prisons," *St. Petersburg Times*, November 18, 2009, sec. Tampa Bay.

14. Alexander Hertel-Fernandez, *Corporate Interests and Conservative Mobilization Across the U.S. States, 1973 to 2013* (PhD diss., Harvard University, 2016), "Chapter 1: The Emergence and Evolution of the Conservative-Corporate Coalition"; Alexander Hertel-Fernandez, "Who Passes Business's 'Model Bills'? Policy Capacity and Corporate Influence in U.S. State Politics," *Perspectives on Politics* 12, no. 3 (September 2014).

15. "CrimeStrike Special Report: Elements for an Effective Criminal Justice System; Justice for the 1990s and Beyond" (Washington, D.C: NRA CrimeStrike, February 7, 1994).

16. Lucy Morgan, "Crime Report Card Gives Florida a Failing Grade Series: The Legislature: [City Edition]," *St. Petersburg Times*, February 23, 1994, sec. Tampa Bay and State; Tampa Today.

17. "Corrections Corporation of America—SourceWatch," accessed July 26, 2015, http://www.sourcewatch.org/index. php/Corrections_Corporation_of_America#Connections_to_ ALEC_and_Harsh_Sentencing_Laws.2C_which_Drove_Up_ CCA.27s_Profits.

18. Gannett News Service, "Study Shows Power of the Pen: More Prisons Mean Less Crime," *The Salt Lake Tribune*, November 2, 1994, sec. Nation-World.

19. Ibid.

20. Scott Keyes, "How Scott Walker Built a Career Sending Wisconsin Inmates to Private Prisons," *The Nation*, February 28, 2015, http://www.thenation.com/article/ how-scott-walker-built-career-sending-wisconsin- inmates-private-prisons/; "Corrections Corporation of America—SourceWatch."

21. Ray Allen, "Effective Corrections Requires More Than Tough Prisons" (American Legislative Exchange Council Issue Analysis, April 2004), cited in "Proven Pro-Family Criminal Justice Policies That Save Families, Save Tax Payers' Money and Improve the Safety of Our Community," Criminal Justice Policy Brief (Texas LULAC State Executive Office, August 2004), 2.

22. Bob Dart, "Legislative Panel Says Crime Rate Is Booming under Light Punishment: [Final Edition]," *Austin American Statesman*, November 3, 1994, sec. News; "Resolution in Support of the Second Chance Act," *ALEC—American Legislative Exchange Council*, accessed July 26, 2015, http://www.alec.org/model-legislation/resolution-in-support- of -the-second-chance-act/.

23. Michael Hough, interview, 2012; Jerry Madden, interview, July 8, 2015; Pat Nolan, interview, July 9, 2015.

24. "Justice Performance Project," *ALEC—American Legislative Exchange Council*, accessed December 4, 2015, http://www.alec. org/task-forces/justice-performance-project/.

25. David Dagan and Steven M. Teles, "The Conservative War on Prisons," *The Washington Monthly*, December 2012, http://www. washingtonmonthly.com/magazine/novemberdecember_2012/ features/the_conservative_war_on_prison041104.php.
26. Michael Hough, interview, June 25, 2015.
27. Ibid.
28. American Legislative Exchange Council, "ALEC Response to Krugman's Erroneous Claims—3/27/12," accessed June 27, 2014, http://www.alec.org/alec-response-krugman%e2%80%99s-erroneous-claims/.
29. Julie Stewart, interview, July 10, 2012.
30. "'Criminal Justice' in Model Legislation," *ALEC—American Legislative Exchange Council*, accessed December 2, 2015, http://www.alec.org/search/criminal+justice/.
31. Alysia Santo, "When Freedom Isn't Free," *Washington Monthly*, May 2015, http://www.washingtonmonthly.com/magazine/ marchaprilmay_2015/features/when_freedom_isnt_free054224. php?page=all.
32. Courtney O'Brien, "35 Day Mailing—2011 Annual Meeting" (American Legislative Exchange Council, June 30, 2011); Courtney O'Brien, "35 Day Mailing-2011 States and Nation Policy Summit" (American Legislative Exchange Council, October 27, 2011).
33. Untitled grant application, Center for Effective Justice, TPPF, n.d.
34. Ibid.
35. Email from Adam Gelb, November 28, 2015.
36. Pat Nolan, interview, July 8, 2015.
37. Newt Gingrich and Pat Nolan, "Prison Reform: A Smart Way for States to Save Money and Lives," *The Washington Post*, January 7, 2011, sec. Opinions, http://www.washingtonpost. com/wp-dyn/content/article/2011/01/06/AR2011010604386. html.
38. "Statement of Principles," *Right on Crime*, accessed July 26, 2015, http://rightoncrime.com/the-conservative-case-for-reform/ statement-of-principles/.
39. Ibid.
40. Untitled grant application, TPPF.

41. Republican Governors Association, "Communication to Republican Gubernatorial Candidates," September 14, 2010; "Reducing Crime and Corrections Spending: Proven Approaches" (The Constitution Project, n.d.).

42. Republican Governors Association, "Communication to Republican Gubernatorial Candidates"; Mary McClymont, Public Welfare Foundation, interview, April 23, 2014.

43. John Buntin, "Mississippi's Corrections Reform," *Governing*, August 2010, http://www.governing.com/topics/public-justice-safety/courts-corrections/mississippi-correction-reform.html.

44. George M. Leader and Matthew J. Brouillette, "Pa. Needs Corrections Reform," *Philly.com*, accessed June 27, 2014, http://articles.philly.com/2012-05-31/news/31923691_1_parole-hearing-process-new-prisons-prison-time.

45. Joseph Coletti, interview, October 2011; Richard Viguerie, interview, March 13, 2012; Justin Keener, interview, phone, March 11, 2014.

46. David Keene, interview, May 9, 2014; Richard Viguerie, interview.

47. Mississippi Senator Willie Simmons, quoted in Buntin, "Mississippi's Corrections Reform"; Jerry Madden, quoted in Carrie Teegardin and Bill Rankin, "Is Price Too High for Punishment?: Long Prison Terms Part of State's Tough Stance. Experts Say Cheaper Alternatives Don't Put Public Safety at Risk," *The Atlanta Journal-Constitution*, May 23, 2010, sec. News.

48. Walter C. Jones, "Ga. Leaders Depend on the Same Well for Ideas," *Savannah Morning News*, October 8, 2012, sec. Georgia.

49. Sarah Reckhow traces the spread of the "failing schools" meme in her book, *Follow the Money: How Foundation Dollars Change Public School Politics* (Oxford: Oxford University Press, 2012).

50. Tony Perkins, interview, July 12, 2012.

51. "Norquist Tells ALEC He Wants U.S. to Revive Decapitation," *The Progressive*, December 30, 2013, http://progressive.org/norquist-tells-alec-he-wants-us-to-revive-decapitation.

52. An unusual, if partial, exception came from ALEC in 2012, when the group issued a statement declaring that its legislator-members are committed to solving key problems and added: "Sometimes that commitment will require us to reevaluate policies and change course. We are not afraid to do so when the facts demand it." American Legislative Exchange Council, "ALEC Response to Krugman's Erroneous Claims—3/27/12."

Chapter 8

1. Bill Rankin, "Criminal Justice Reform Panel to Continue Its Work: Governor Signs Order, Directs Council to Report Findings by Year's End," *The Atlanta Journal-Constitution*, May 26, 2012; Aaron Gould Sheinin and Bill Rankin, "After the Legislature: Jail Reform Law Signed: $264 Million Expected to Be Saved in 5 Years. Options to Prison Time Will Be Offered for Nonviolent Offenses," *The Atlanta Journal-Constitution*, May 3, 2012, sec. B1.
2. Neil King Jr., "As Prisons Squeeze Budgets, GOP Rethinks Crime Focus," *Wall Street Journal*, June 21, 2013, http://www.wsj.com/news/articles/SB10001424127887323836504578551902602217018.
3. Ibid.; Nathan Deal, interview, August 5, 2015.
4. Robert Martinson, "What Works: Questions and Answers About Prison Reform," *The Public Interest*, no. 35, Spring 1974, pp. 22–54.
5. The Pew Center on the States, "One in 31: The Long Reach of American Corrections" (Washington, D.C: The Pew Charitable Trusts, March 2009).
6. Thomas Worthy, interview, June 6, 2015.
7. Jay Neal, interview, December 6, 2013.
8. Ibid.
9. Ibid.
10. Ibid.
11. Ibid.
12. Kelly McCutchen, interview, December 13, 2004.
13. Bill Crane, "Georgia View: Locking Up the Bad Guys," *Georgia Trend*, March 2012, http://www.georgiatrend.com/March-2012/Georgia-View-Locking-Up-The-Bad-Guys/.

14. The Pew Center on the States, "One in 31: The Long Reach of American Corrections."

15. Stacey Abrams, interview, June 18, 2015.

16. Ray Henry, "Republicans Nearing Supermajority in Georgia Legislature," *The Augusta Chronicle*, October 13, 2012, http://chronicle.augusta.com/news/government/2012-10-13/republicans-nearing-supermajority-georgia-legislature.

17. Ray Henry and Shannon McCaffrey, "Republicans Surge in Georgia Takeover," Associated Press, November 4, 2010; Brandon Howell, "Kidd Denies State House GOP Supermajority," *Georgia Tipsheet*, 2012, http://georgiatipsheet.com/2012/11/30/kidd-denies-state-house-gop-supermajority/.

18. Nathan Deal, "Inaugural Address of Governor Nathan Deal" (Atlanta, GA, January 10, 2011), http://gov.georgia.gov/press-releases/2011-01-10/inaugural-address-governor-nathan-deal.

19. Worthy, interview, June 6, 2015.

20. Michael Thompson, "Justice Reinvestment White Paper," n.d.

21. "Leading on Public Safety: 4 Governors Share Lessons Learned from Sentencing and Corrections Reform," Public Safety Performance Project (The Pew Charitable Trusts, August 2013), http://www.pewtrusts.org/~/media/legacy/uploadedfiles/pcs_assets/2013/PewPSPPGovernorsQApdf.pdf; Michael Thompson, interview, January 6, 2015.

22. Radley Balko, "Good Riddance, Mr. McDade," *The Washington Post*, April 4, 2014, http://www.washingtonpost.com/news/the-watch/wp/2014/04/04/good-riddance-mr-mcdade/.

23. Worthy, interview, June 6, 2015.

24. Carrie Teegardin and Bill Rankin, "Legislative Preview: Georgia Rethinks Prison Stance: Lock-'Em-up Philosophy Might Be Replaced with 'Smart-on-Crime' Strategy," *The Atlanta Journal-Constitution*, January 3, 2012.

25. Abrams, interview.

26. Rich Golick, interview, June 17, 2015.

27. Walter C. Jones, "Criminal-Justice Reform Awaits Committee OK," *Savannah Morning News*, March 12, 2012; Carrie Teegardin and Bill Rankin, "Legislature 2012: Prison Reform Takes 1st Step: Governor Not on Board with Bill That Backers Say Will Save Millions," *The Atlanta Journal-Constitution*, February 28, 2012.

28. Bill Rankin, "Sentencing Plan Advances: Sweeping Changes to Criminal Justice Laws Get Committee's OK," *The Atlanta Journal-Constitution*, March 21, 2012.

29. Thomas Worthy, interview, July 2, 2015.

30. Golick, interview.

31. The Pew Center on the States, "2012 Georgia Public Safety Reform," Public Safety Performance Project (Washington, D.C: The Pew Charitable Trusts, July 2012); "Report of the Georgia Council on Criminal Justice Reform," January 2014, https://gov. georgia.gov/sites/gov.georgia.gov/files/related_files/document/ GA%20Criminal%20Justice%20Reform%20Council%20Report. pdf; Thomas Worthy, July 16, 2015; Adam Gelb, December 1, 2015;. Accountability courts were also permitted to charge their wards up to $1,000, up from the previous maximum of $300. *Georgia State University Law Review; Volume 29, Issue 1, Fall 2012, Article 15. The piece is titled "Crimes and Offenses HB 1176.*

32. "Report of the Special Council on Criminal Justice Reform for Georgians," November 2011, http://www.legis.ga.gov/ Documents/GACouncilReport-FINALDRAFT.pdf.

33. Jones, "Criminal-Justice Reform Awaits Committee OK"; "Public Attitudes on Crime and Punishment in Georgia," *The Pew Charitable Trusts*, February 24, 2012, http://www.pewtrusts. org/en/research-and-analysis/reports/0001/01/01/public-atti-tudes-on-crime-and-punishment-in-georgia; Adam Gelb e-mail to David Dagan, November 8, 2015.

34. Newt Gingrich and Kelly McCutchen, "Georgia Can Lead Again on Juvenile Justice Reform," *The Marietta Daily Journal*, March 20, 2013, http://mdjonline.com/view/full_story/ 22019205/article-Georgia-can-lead-again-on-juvenile-justice-reform?instance=secondary_story_left_column.

35. Pat Nolan, interview, July 8, 2015.

36. Abrams, interview.

37. Teegardin and Rankin, "Legislative Preview: Georgia Rethinks Prison Stance: Lock-'Em-Up Philosophy Might Be Replaced with 'Smart-on-Crime' Strategy."

38. Worthy, interview, June 6, 2015.

39. Golick, interview.

40. Worthy, interview, June 6, 2015.

41. Golick, interview.
42. Chuck Spahos, interview, December 16, 2013.
43. Public Safety Performance Project, "Bipartisan Support for Justice Reinvestment Legislation" (Washington, D.C: The Pew Charitable Trusts, June 17, 2015), http://bit.ly/1FfCJeT.
44. Abrams, interview.
45. Neal, interview, December 6, 2013.
46. Public Safety Performance Project, "Georgia's 2013 Juvenile Justice Reform" (Washington, D.C: The Pew Charitable Trusts, July 2013), http://bit.ly/1FD6ztr.
47. Wendell Willard et al., *Courts; Juvenile Proceedings; Substantially Revise, Supersede, and Modernize Provisions*, 2013, http://www.legis.ga.gov/legislation/en-US/Display/20132014/HB/242.
48. Mike Klein, "Second Adult Criminal Justice Reform Bill Becomes Law," Georgia Public Policy Foundation (April 25, 2013), http://www.georgiapolicy.org/2013/04/second-adult-criminal-justice-reform-bill-becomes-law/.
49. Jesse Stone et al., *Fair Business Practices Act; Enact Offender Reentry Reforms as Recommended by the Georgia Council on Criminal Justice Reform*, 2014, http://www.legis.ga.gov/Legislation/en-US/display/20132014/SB/365.
50. Reid Wilson, "Georgia the Latest State to 'Ban the Box' in Hiring Practices," *The Washington Post*, February 24, 2015, https://www.washingtonpost.com/blogs/govbeat/wp/2015/02/24/georgia-the-latest-state-to-ban-the-box-in-hiring-practices/.
51. Carrie Teegardin, "House Committee Approves Probation Reform Bill," *The Atlanta Journal-Constitution*, March 3, 2015, http://investigations.blog.ajc.com/2015/03/02/house-committee-approves-probation-reform-bill/; Jonathan Phillips, "Education at Heart of Georgia's Next Wave of Change in Criminal Justice," *The Atlanta Journal-Constitution*, April 19, 2015, http://www.ajc.com/news/news/state-regional-govt-politics/education-at-heart-of-georgias-next-wave-of-change/nkt5W/; Michael W. Nail, "Department of Community Supervision: Georgia's Newest State Agency," Georgia.gov (June 30, 2015), https://georgia.gov/blog/2015-06-30/department-community-supervision-georgias-newest-state-agency.

52. Judge Michael P. Boggs and Thomas Worthy, "Report of the Georgia Council on Criminal Justice Reform," February 2015; Rich Golick et al., *Criminal Cases; Provide State with More Direct Appeal Rights; Provisions*, n.d., http://www.legis.ga.gov/legislation/en-US/display/20132014/HB/349.

53. Worthy, interview, June 6, 2015.

54. Walter C. Jones, "Senate OKs Effort to Assist Freed Inmates: Transition from Prison to Freedom Focus of One of Deal's Reforms," *Florida Times-Union*, March 22, 2014.

55. Abrams, interview.

56. Boggs and Worthy, "Report of the Georgia Council on Criminal Justice Reform."

57. Golick, interview.

58. Greg Bluestein, "Charter Schools for Prisons Part of Plan: Governor Proposes More than $12M for Re-Entry Programs," *The Atlanta Journal-Constitution*, January 23, 2015.

59. Bill Rankin and Aaron Gould Sheinin, "Ga. Sending Fewer Blacks to Prison: Courts, Sentencing, Drug Culture See Changes," *The Atlanta Journal-Constitution*, August 3, 2014.

60. Eric Stirgus, "Sentencing Changes Yield a Financial Boon for Georgia," *The Atlanta Journal-Constitution*, March 19, 2014; Marcus E. Howard, "State Inmate Subsidies to Rise," *Savannah Morning News*, March 17, 2014.

61. Andrew Cohen, "The Petri Dish: Georgia Has Become the Laboratory of Criminal Justice Reform," *The Marshall Project*, March 19, 2015, https://www.themarshallproject.org/2015/03/19/the-petri-dish.

62. Naomi Shavin, "A Republican Governor Is Leading the Country's Most Successful Prison Reform," *The New Republic*, March 31, 2015, http://www.newrepublic.com/article/121425/gop-governor-nathan-deal-leading-us-prison-reform; "Agenda," *Bipartisan Summit on Criminal Justice Reform*, accessed June 28, 2015, http://www.bipartisansummit.org/agenda.html.

63. Worthy, interview, June 6, 2015.

64. Neil King Jr., "As Prisons Squeeze Budgets, GOP Rethinks Crime Focus".

65. Greg Bluestein and Jeremy Redmon, "Governor's Race: Victory Gives Deal 4 More Years: Incumbent Scores Convincing Win in Bitter Clash of Ideals with Jason Carter," *The Atlanta Journal-Constitution*, November 5, 2014.

66. "Political Insider: Nathan Deal Pivots to Black Voters in Election's Final Days," *Atlanta Journal—Constitution Blogs*, October 31, 2014.

67. Abrams, interview.

68. Neal, interview, December 6, 2013.

69. Greg Bluestein, "Justice System: Faith Gets Role in Justice Reform: Deal Pressing Religious Groups to Mentor Ex-Cons Who Struggle," *The Atlanta Journal—Constitution*, July 7, 2014.

70. "AJC: Deal's Criminal Justice Reforms Paying Dividends," *Office of the Governor*, August 4, 2014, http://gov.georgia.gov/press-releases/2014-08-04/ajc-deals-criminal-justice-reforms-paying-dividends.

71. Deal, "Inaugural Address of Governor Nathan Deal."

72. Worthy, interview, June 6, 2015.

73. Marie Gottschalk, *Caught: The Prison State and the Lockdown of American Politics* (Princeton, NJ: Princeton University Press, 2014); Christopher Seeds, "Bifurcation Nation: Strategy in Contemporary American Punishment," June 19, 2015; Nathan Deal, "One-Size-Fits-All Doesn't Always Serve Justice," *The Atlanta Journal-Constitution*, February 24, 2013.

74. Danny Porter, interview, July 16, 2015.

75. "James Oglethorpe (1696–1785)," *New Georgia Encyclopedia*, accessed July 27, 2015, http://www.georgiaencyclopedia.org/articles/history-archaeology/james-oglethorpe-1696-1785.

76. Shavin, "A Republican Governor Is Leading the Country's Most Successful Prison Reform."

77. "Mississippi's 2014 Corrections and Criminal Justice Reform: Legislation to Improve Public Safety, Ensure Certainty in Sentencing, and Control Corrections Costs" (Pew Charitable Trusts, May 2014), http://bit.ly/1CLywBS; Buntin, "Mississippi's Corrections Reform."

78. Marc Kovac, "Governor Signs Sentencing Reform Bill," *The Daily Record*, July 3, 2011, http://www.the-daily-record.com/local%20news/2011/07/03/governor-signs-sentencing-reform-bill; Joe Guillen, "New Ohio Criminal Sentencing Bill to Save Millions by Letting Inmates Out Early, Sending Low-Level Felons to Prison Alternatives," *The Plain Dealer*, June 27, 2011, http://www.cleveland.com/open/index.ssf/2011/06/new_ohio_criminal_sentencing_l.html; David J. Diroll, "H.B. 86 Summary: The 2011 Changes to

Criminal and Juvenile Law: August 2011 Draft" (Columbus, Ohio: Ohio Criminal Sentencing Commission, August 2011).

79. Associated Press, "Perdue Signs DWI, Probation and Prison Laws," *FayObserver.com*, accessed November 22, 2013, http://fayobserver.com/articles/2011/06/23/1103872; James Markham, "Justice Reinvestment Essentials Chart" (Chapel Hill, NC: UNC School of Government, 2012), "Justice Reinvestment Act: Historic Progress for Correction," Correction News (North Carolina Department of Correction, July 2011), http://www.doc.state.nc.us/Newsletter/JRnewsletter.pdf; "Justice Reinvestment in North Carolina: How North Carolina Is Reducing Corrections Costs and Recidivism" (Council of State Governments Justice Center, December 15, 2011), http://csgjusticecenter.org/jr/nc/.

80. Paul Alongi, "Plan to Cut Sentences for Nonviolent Offenders Could Save Taxpayers Millions," *The Greenville News*, February 22, 2010; Jason Spencer, "Sanford Backs Plan to Put Fewer Non-Violent Offenders in Prison," *Spartanburg Herald Journal*, April 22, 2010, http://www.goupstate.com/article/20100422/ARTICLES/4221030; "South Carolina's Public Safety Reform: Legislation Enacts Research-Based Strategies to Cut Prison Growth and Costs" (The Pew Center on the States, June 2010), http://www.pewtrusts.org/en/research-and-analysis/reports/2010/07/06/south-carolinas-public-safety-reform.

81. John Buntin, "Mississippi's Corrections Reform," *Governing*, August 2010, http://www.governing.com/topics/public-justice-safety/courts-corrections/mississippi-correction-reform.html.

82. "Final Report: Mississippi Corrections and Criminal Justice Task Force," December 2013, 5, http://www.legislature.ms.gov/Documents/MSTaskForce_FinalReport.pdf.

83. "Mississippi," *Bureau of Justice Assistance: Justice Reinvestment Initiative*, n.d., https://www.bja.gov/programs/justicereinvestment/mississippi.html; "Mississippi Enacts Comprehensive, Bipartisan Criminal Justice Reforms," *Mississippi's 64th Governor, Phil Bryant*, March 31, 2014, http://www.governorbryant.com/mississippi-enacts-comprehensive-bipartisan-criminal-justice-reforms/.

84. Tate Reeves (Right on Crime Leadership Summit, Washington, D.C., May 21, 2014).

85. Brice Wiggins (Right on Crime Leadership Summit, Washington, D.C., May 21, 2014).

86. James Varney, "For Louisiana Criminal Justice Reform, the Time Is Now," *NOLA.com*, April 1, 2014, http://www.nola.com/opinions/index.ssf/2014/04/for_louisiana_and_criminal_jus.html; see also Jarvis DeBerry, "Mass Incarceration Is a Problem Louisiana Chief Justice Bernette Johnson Wants Fixed," *The Times-Picayune*, May 12, 2015, http://www.nola.com/crime/index.ssf/2015/05/mass_incarceration_louisiana.html.

87. Alison Lawrence, "Justice Reinvestment: Louisiana," *National Conference of State Legislators*, October 3, 2014, http://www.ncsl.org/research/civil-and-criminal-justice/justice-reinvestment-in-louisiana.aspx.

88. Allison DeFoor e-mail to Steven Teles, April 16, 2015; Times-Union Editorial, "Georgia Is Far Ahead of Florida on Prison Reform," *The Florida Times-Union*, April 1, 2015, http://jacksonville.com/opinion/editorials/2015-04-01/story/georgia-far-ahead-florida-prison-reform.

Chapter 9

1. "Reno Backs Strict Sentences for Sellers of Crack Cocaine," *The New York Times*, April 16, 1995.

2. Pat Nolan, interview, April 19, 2011.

3. Harry Reid, "S.206—105th Congress (1997–1998)," legislation (March 19, 1997), https://www.congress.gov/bill/105th-congress/senate-bill/206/text.

4. Pat Nolan, interview, August 6, 2012; Clyde Weiss, "Ex-Nixon Aide Argues against Reid Bill: [Final Edition]," *Las Vegas Review-Journal*, May 14, 1997, sec. B.

5. Philip Parker, "Religious-Freedom Bill Tentatively OK'd," *Amarillo Globe-News*, May 18, 1999, http://amarillo.com/stories/1999/05/18/tex_bill.shtml#.Vl5SjN-rSfU.

6. *City of Boerne v. Flores, Archbishop of San Antonio et al.* (521 U.S. 507 1997).

7. "We Hold These Truths: A Statement of Christian Conscience and Citizenship," October 1997, http://www.firstthings.com/article/1997/10/004-we-hold-these-truths.

8. U.S. Government Printing Office, *Religious Land Use and Institutionalized Persons Act of 2000*, vol. 42, U.S.C § 2000cc, 2000, http://www.gpo.gov/fdsys/pkg/PLAW-106publ274/html/PLAW-106publ274.htm; *Protecting Religious Freedom After Boerne v. Flores* (U.S. Government Printing Office, 1997); Charles T. Canady, *Religious Liberty Protection Act of 1998*, 1998, http://www.justice.gov/sites/default/files/jmd/legacy/2014/01/13/hear-134-1998.pdf.

9. "Religious Liberty Protection Act of 1999" (145 Cong Rec H 5580, July 15, 1999).

10. Steven M. Teles, "Conservative Public Interest Law I: Mistakes Made," in *The Rise of the Conservative Legal Movement* (Princeton, NJ: Princeton University Press, 2008).

11. Michael Horowitz, interview, June 19, 2012.

12. "Bill Summary and Status 108th Congress (2003–2004) H.R. 1707" (The Library of Congress, n.d.), http://thomas.loc.gov/cgi-bin/bdquery/z?d108:HR01707.

13. Frank Wolf, interview, July 20, 2015; Frank R. Wolf, "Chuck Was a Giant . . . ," *BreakPoint*, May 6, 2013, http://www.breakpoint.org/founders-vision-blog/entry/54/22164.

14. Email from Ed Haden to David Dagan, June 17, 2015.

15. Robert Toone, interview, June 28, 2012; Robert Toone, interview, June 21, 2012.

16. Jacob Sullum, "Prison Conversion," *Reason* 31, no. 4 (September 8, 1999): 40.

17. Pamela K. Lattimore et al., "Implementation of Prisoner Reentry Programs: Findings from the Serious and Violent Offender Reentry Initiative Multi-Site Evaluation," *Justice Research and Policy* 7, no. 2 (December 1, 2005): 87–109.

18. Gene Guerrero, interview, June 25, 2012. Also Gene Guerrero to rfield@voa.org et al., "Next Conf Call Re: Danny Davis Housing for Ex Offenders Bill—Friday, February 21 at 3:30 PM," February 14, 2003; Gene Guerrero to Susan Tucker, Jo-Ann Mort, and Nkechi Taifa, "Reentry Legislation," May 14, 2004; Charles Sullivan to Gary Fields et al., "Second Chance Act,"

October 16, 2006; Reentry Working Group, "Suggestions for the Refinement and Promotion of the Second Chance Act of 2004," December 17, 2004; Jessica Nickel, interview, March 18, 2015.

19. Pat Nolan, interview, July 20, 2015; Sam Brownback, *Second Chance Act of 2004*, 2004, https://www.congress.gov/bill/108th-congress/senate-bill/2789?q=%7B%22search%22%3A%5B%22sam+brownback%22%5D%7D.

20. "Congressional Record Daily Edition, Second Chance Act" (154 Cong Rec S 2938, April 10, 2008).

21. David Keene, interview, November 4, 2015.

22. Nickel, interview.

23. Ed Haden, interview, June 27, 2012.

24. Nickel, interview.

25. "Kansas Forms New Partnership to Take on Recidivism," *Right on Crime*, accessed July 27, 2015, http://rightoncrime.com/2011/06/kansas-forms-new-partnership-to-take-on-recidivism/; "Kansas Abolishes Its Parole Board," *Right on Crime*, accessed July 27, 2015, http://rightoncrime.com/2011/04/kansas-abolishes-its-parole-board/.

26. James Bovard, "The Dangerous Expansion of Forfeiture Laws," *Wall Street Journal*, December 29, 1997, sec. Front Section, http://www.wsj.com/articles/SB883336648778803000; James Bovard, "Take It Away—Popularized by the War on Drugs, Asset Forfeiture Has Been Expanded to Cover More and More Offenses—Whether Proven or Not. Soon No One's Property Will Be Safe," *National Review*, 1995; James Bovard, "New Assault on Property Rights," *Washington Times*, October 24, 1996; Scripps News Service, "Property Forfeiture Laws Targeted by Hyde," March 10, 1999; Frank A. Aukofer, "Bill to Overhaul Asset Forfeiture Laws Unites a Very Odd Group of Bedfellows," *Milwaukee Journal Sentinel*, May 14, 1999.

27. David Keene, "An Odd Coalition Is Fighting Asset Forfeiture," *The Hill*, May 5, 1999.

28. Karen Dillon, "States' Forfeiture Woes Trace to Federal Officials," *The Kansas City Star*, May 22, 2000, Metropolitan edition.

29. Karen Dillon, "Police, Federal Agencies Resist Change—States, Critics Look to Washington to Stop Hand-Offs," *The*

Kansas City Star, May 22, 2000, Metropolitan edition. Fifteen years later, Senate Judiciary Chairman Chuck Grassley—a longtime crime hardliner—observed that in 2000, "the most important procedural reforms were gutted at the behest of law enforcement." "Sen. Charles E. Grassley Holds a Hearing on the Need to Reform Asset Forfeiture," *Congressional Quarterly Transcriptions,* April 15, 2015.

30. "Part I: Policing for Profit," *Policing for Profit* (Institute for Justice, March 2010), https://ij.org/report/policing-for-profit-first-edition/part-i-policing-for-profit/.

31. Scott Bullock, interview, July 21, 2015; Radley Balko, *Rise of the Warrior Cop: The Militarization of America's Police Forces* (New York: PublicAffairs, 2013).

32. Paul Rosenzweig and Brian W. Walsh, *One Nation Under Arrest: How Crazy Laws, Rogue Prosecutors, and Activist Judges Threaten Your Liberty* (Washington, D.C: The Heritage Foundation, 2010); Paul Rosenzweig, "The Over-Criminalization of Social and Economic Conduct" (The Heritage Foundation, April 17, 2003), http://www.heritage.org/research/reports/2003/04/the-over-criminalization-of-social-and-economic-conduct; Brian W. Walsh, "Doing Violence to the Law: The Over-Federalization of Crime," Commentary on Legal Issues, Rule of Law (The Heritage Foundation, June 9, 2011), http://www.heritage.org/research/commentary/2011/06/doing-violence-to-the-law-the-over-federalization-of-crime.

33. Senate Hearing 105-154, "Medicare at Risk: Emerging Fraud in Medicare Programs," Committee on Governmental Affairs, Permanent Subcommittee on Investigations, June 26, 1997; Statement of Ed Meese, Senate Hearing 105-305, "Environmental Audits," Committee on Environment and Public Works, Oct. 30, 1997. House Hearing 109-87, "America's Capital Markets: Maintaining Our Lead in the 21st Century," Committee on Financial Services, Subcommittee on Capital Markets, Insurance, and Government Sponsored Enterprises, April 26, 2006.

34. Brian W. Walsh, interview, December 31, 2013.

35. Roy Wenzl, "Charles Koch's Views on Criminal Justice System Just May Surprise You," *The Wichita Eagle,* December

27, 2014, http://www.kansas.com/news/special-reports/koch/
article5050731.html. The Kochs only became public about
their concerns after criminal justice had already become a
hot topic on the right, but in fact, David Koch has been a
longtime donor to Families Against Mandatory Minimums.
Julie Stewart, "A Perfect Storm for Sentencing Reform,"
MSNBC, August 16, 2013, http://www.msnbc.com/msnbc/
perfect-storm-sentencing-reform.

36. Brian W. Walsh, interview, November 24, 2015; Pat Nolan,
interview, June 18, 2015.

37. Brian W. Walsh, interview, November 13, 2015.

38. Statement of Stephen A. Saltzburg, on behalf of the American
Bar Association, "Over-Criminalization of Conduct/Over-
Federalization of Criminal Law," House Hearing 111-67,
Judiciary Committee, Subcommittee on Crime, Terrorism, and
Homeland Security, July 22, 2009.

39. House Hearing 111-151, "Reining in Over-Criminalization,"
Judiciary Committee, Subcommittee on Crime, Terrorism, and
Homeland Security, Sept. 28, 2010.

40. "Labrador & Scott Introduce Bipartisan Bill to Reform
Criminal Sentencing Laws," *Congressman Raul Labrador*, October
30, 2013, https://labrador.house.gov/press-releases/labrador-
scott-introduce-bipartisan-bill-to-reform-criminal-sentencing
-laws/; "Reps. Scott, Massie Introduce Justice Safety Valve
Act," *Congressman Thomas Massie*, (April 24, 2013), http://massie.
house.gov/press-release/press-release-reps-
scott-massie-introduce-justice-safety-valve-act.

41. Robert Scott, *H.R. 3327—111th Congress (2009–2010): Ramos-
Compean Justice Act of 2009*, 2009, https://www.congress.gov/
bill/111th-congress/house-bill/3327.

42. "Chaffetz, Scott Work to Improve Federal Prison System,"
Congressman Jason Chaffetz, July 11, 2013, https://chaffetz.
house.gov/press-release/chaffetz-scott-work-improve-federal-
prison-system; "Lawmakers Introduce Bipartisan Bill to
Reform Federal Prison System," *Congressman Jason Chaffetz*,
February 5, 2015, https://chaffetz.house.gov/press-release/
lawmakers-introduce-bipartisan-bill-reform-federal-prison-
system; "Bipartisan House Coalition Launches Caucus Aimed
at Criminal Justice Reform," *Congressman Jason Chaffetz*, July 15,

2015, https://chaffetz.house.gov/press-release/bipartisan-house-coalition-launches-caucus-aimed-criminal-justice-reform.

43. Gannett News Service, "Bill to Target Cocaine Sentencing Gap," September 6, 2001; Gary Fields, "U.S. Senators Rethink Cocaine Laws—Conservative Lawmakers Seek to Narrow Disparities in Sentencing Rules," *Wall Street Journal*, January 15, 2002.

44. Pat Nolan, interview, August 6, 2012; endorsements listed in "Fair Sentencing Act of 2010" (*Congressional Record* Daily Edition, 2010); Pat Nolan, "Reform Means Fairness: House Vote Would End Disparity in Crack Sentencing," *Washington Times*, July 23, 2010, sec. Commentary.

45. The leaders were Families Against Mandatory Minimums and the left-leaning Open Society Institute and Criminal Justice Policy Foundation. Pat Nolan, August 6, 2012; *Fair Sentencing Act of 2010* (*Congressional Record* Daily Edition, 2010); Pat Nolan, "Reform Means Fairness: House Vote Would End Disparity in Crack Sentencing," *Washington Times*, July 23, 2010, sec. Commentary.

46. Pat Nolan et al. to John A. Boehner, May 25, 2010, http://bit.ly/1LDqLCn.

47. Julie Stewart, interview, July 10, 2012.

48. The three Republican cosponsors were Senators Lindsey Graham, Orrin Hatch, and Olympia Snowe. "S.714—National Criminal Justice Commission Act of 2010," (March 26, 2009), http://thomas.loc.gov/cgi-bin/bdquery/z?d111:SN00714:@@@P.

49. David Rogers, "Republicans Block Justice Review Proposal in Senate," *Politico*, October 20, 2011, http://www.politico.com/news/stories/1011/66491.html.

50. Yet another commission was proposed in the Senate in 2015, with bipartisan support. Gary Peters, *National Criminal Justice Commission Act of 2015*, 2015, https://www.congress.gov/bill/114th-congress/senate-bill/1119/cosponsors.

51. In late 2014, Scott issued a lengthy minority report that amounted to a full-blown critique of the federal justice system.

52. Bobby Scott, interview, November 24, 2015.

53. "Marc Levin Testimony at House Judiciary Committee Overcriminalization Task Force," *Right on Crime*, May 30, 2014,

http://rightoncrime.com/2014/05/marc-levin-testimony-at-house-judiciary-committee-overcriminalization-task-force/.

54. Adam Gelb e-mail to David Dagan, December 6, 2015.

55. Karen J. Cohen, "Mandatory Prison Terms Are Unfair, Panel Told," *Wisconsin State Journal*, July 29, 1993, sec. Front.

56. "How Wisconsin Delegation Voted on Key Issues," *USA Today*, April 6, 1995; Marcy Gordon, "House Passes GOP Crime Bill," *The Capital Times*, February 11, 2015, sec. Nation/World.

57. Michael Kirkland, "Sensenbrenner Rakes Judges over Coals," *UPI NewsTrack*, March 16, 2004, sec. News.

58. Debra J. Saunders, "The New Inquisitor," *San Francisco Chronicle*, July 17, 2005, Final edition, sec. Editorial.

59. Nickel, interview.

60. Anand Giridharadas, "Momentum on Criminal Justice Repair," *The New York Times*, June 22, 2015, http://www.nytimes.com/2015/06/23/us/momentum-on-criminal-justice-repair.html.

61. American Enterprise Institute, *How Can We Have Less Crime and Less Incarceration?*, 2015, https://www.youtube.com/watch?v=MgIoyb4CONg.

62. "Bipartisan Summit on Criminal Justice Reform," accessed August 31, 2015, http://www.bipartisansummit.org/.

63. "About the Coalition for Public Safety," *Coalition for Public Safety*, accessed December 6, 2015, http://www.coalitionfor-publicsafety.org/about/.

64. David Dagan, "Paul Ryan Could Take the Easy Road on Criminal Justice Reform. He Shouldn't," *The Huffington Post*, January 12, 2016, http://www.huffingtonpost.com/david-dagan/paul-ryan-easy-road-criminal-justice_b_8962592.html.

65. Steven M. Teles, "The Eternal Return of Compassionate Conservatism," *National Affairs*, no. 1 (Fall 2009), http://www.nationalaffairs.com/publications/detail/the-eternal-return-of-compassionate-conservatism.

66. Igor Bobic, "Rand Paul Pushes for Criminal Justice Reform at Historically Black College," *Huffington Post*, March 13, 2015, http://www.huffingtonpost.com/2015/03/13/rand-paul-criminal-justice-reform_n_6866702.htm.

67. Rick Perry, "Rick Perry on Economic Opportunity Creation" (National Press Club, July 2, 2015), http://www.c-span.org/

video/?326898-1/former-governor-rick-perry-rtx-economic-plan; Rick Perry, "Rick Perry, the Former Three-Term Governor of Texas and a 2016 Presidential Candidate, Will Lay Out an Economic Plan" (National Press Club, Washington D.C., July 2, 2015), https://www.press.org/sites/default/files/20150702_perry.pdf.

68. Eliza Collins, "Cruz: 'Overwhelming Majority of Violent Criminals Are Democrats,'" *Politico*, November 30, 2015, http://social.politico.com/story/2015/11/ted-cruz-planned-parenthood-democrats-crime-216288; Mary Clare Jalonick, "Senate Bill Could Cut Nonviolent Drug Offenders' Sentences," *The Associated Press*, October 22, 2015, http://bigstory.ap.org/article/c7f94291980c4c22b-0216106d2a8de4b/senate-bill-could-cut-nonviolent-drug-offenders-sentences; David Dagan, "The Tea Party Gets Something Right," *The Washington Monthly—Ten Miles Square*, January 31, 2014, http://www.washington-monthly.com/ten-miles-square/2014/01/the_tea_party_gets_something_r048873.php; Seung Min Kim, "Cotton Leads Effort to Sink Sentencing Overhaul," *Politico*, January 25, 2016, http://www.politico.com/story/2016/01/criminal-justice-tom-cotton-218121.

Chapter 10

1. John T. Bennett, "The Sequester, the Pentagon, and the Little Campaign That Could," New America's Strange Bedfellows Series (New America Foundation, September 2015), https://static.newamerica.org/attachments/9826-the-sequester-the-pentagon-and-the-little-campaign-that-could/PentagonBudgetReform_Option2.6de75538a2884e019cobbf1cb78cfae2.pdf

2. Lydia Bean and Steve Teles, "Spreading the Gospel of Climate Change: An Evangelical Battleground," New America's Strange Bedfellows Series (New America Foundation, November 2015), https://static.newamerica.org/attachments/11649-spreading-the-gospel-of-climate-change/climate_care11.9.4f0142a50aa24a2ba65020f7929f6fd7.pdf.

3. Steven M. Teles, *The Rise of the Conservative Legal Movement: The Battle for Control of the Law* (Princeton, NJ: Princeton University Press, 2012).

4. Bean and Teles, "Spreading the Gospel of Climate Change: An Evangelical Battleground."

5. *Bipartisan Discussion on Criminal Justice Reform with Newt Gingrich and Van Jones* (Pew Charitable Trusts, 2010), http://bit.ly/12gvPdI.

6. E. Ann Carson, "Prisoners in 2013" (U.S. Department of Justice, Bureau of Justice Statistics, September 30, 2014), 16, http://www.bjs.gov/content/pub/pdf/p13.pdf.

7. Piper Janoe, "Justice Reinvestment in Oklahoma" (Unpublished manuscript, 2015).

8. Jenna Portnoy, Matt Zapotosky, and Laura Vozzella, "McAuliffe Creates Commission to Study Bringing Parole Back to Virginia," *The Washington Post*, June 24, 2015, http://www.washingtonpost.com/local/virginia-politics/mcauliffe-creates-commission-to-study-bringing-parole-back-to-virginia/2015/06/24/1a10c106-1a7b-11e5-bd7f-4611a60dd8e5_story.html.

9. Jennie Rodriguez-Moore, "Maldonado: Build More Facilities to Fix Prisons," *McClatchy-Tribune Business News*, May 17, 2013.

10. "Addicted to Courts: How a Growing Dependence on Drug Courts Impacts People and Communities" (Justice Policy Institute, March 2011), http://www.justicepolicy.org/uploads/justicepolicy/documents/addicted_to_courts_final.pdf.

11. Robert Weisberg and Joan Petersilia, "The Dangers of Pyrrhic Victories against Mass Incarceration," *Daedalus* 139, no. 3 (Summer 2010): 129.

12. Alysia Santo, "When Freedom Isn't Free," *The Washington Monthly*, May 2015, http://www.washingtonmonthly.com/magazine/marchaprilmay_2015/features/when_freedom_isnt_free054224.php?page=all.

13. Kristen Soltis Anderson, *The Selfie Vote: Where Millennials Are Leading America (and How Republicans Can Keep Up)* (New York: Broadside Books, 2015).

14. R. Kent Weaver, *Ending Welfare as We Know It* (Washington, DC: Brookings Institution Press, 2000).

15. Charles Wilson and Tom Davies, "Daniels' Plan on Indiana Sentencing Changes Seems Dead," *Chesterton Tribune*, April 13, 2011, http://chestertontribune.com/Indiana%20News/daniels_plan_on_indiana_sentenci.htm.

16. Jeffrey T. Ulmer and Darrell Steffensmeier, "The Age and Crime Relationship: Social Variation, Social Explanations," in *The Nurture versus Biosocial Debate in Criminology* (Newbury Park, CA: Sage, 2014), 377–96, http://www.sagepub.com/sites/default/files/upm-binaries/60294_Chapter_23.pdf.

17. Leon Neyfakh, "Cory Booker and Newt Gingrich Want to Redefine What Is Considered a 'Violent' Crime," *Slate*, March 26, 2015, http://www.slate.com/blogs/the_slatest/2015/03/26/bipartisan_summit_on_criminal_justice_reform_cory_booker_wants_to_redefine.html.

18. Luke Millins, "The Battle for the Cato Institute," *The Washingtonian*, May 30, 2012, http://www.washingtonian.com/articles/people/the-battle-for-cato/.

Index